CISTERCIAN STUDIES SERIES: NUMBER TWO HUNDRED FIFTY-TWO

Palladius of Aspuna

The Lausiac History

CISTERCIAN STUDIES SERIES: NUMBER TWO HUNDRED FIFTY-TWO

Palladius of Aspuna

The Lausiac History

Translated by

John Wortley

Cistercian Publications
www.cistercianpublications.org

LITURGICAL PRESS
Collegeville, Minnesota
www.litpress.org

A Cistercian Publications title published by Liturgical Press

Cistercian Publications
Editorial Offices
161 Grosvenor Street
Athens, Ohio 45701
www.cistercianpublications.org

This work is a translation of G. J. M. Bartelink's edition of *Palladio, La Storia Lausiaca* (Milan: Fondazione Lorenza Valla and Libri Mondador, 1974).

Scripture quotations are the translator's own work, with all quotations from the Old Testament based on the Septuagint.

Library of Congress Cataloging-in-Publication Data

Palladius, Bishop of Aspuna, -approximately 430.
[Lausiac history. English]
Palladius of Aspuna : the Lausiac history / translated by John Wortley.
pages cm. — (Cistercian studies series ; number two hundred fifty-two)
Translation compiled from a variety of sources.
Includes bibliographical references.
ISBN 978-0-87907-252-0 — ISBN 978-0-87907-681-8 (ebook)
1. Monasticism and religious orders—Egypt—History—Early church, ca. 30-600. 2. Christian biography—Egypt—Early works to 1800. I. Wortley, John, translator. II. Title.

BX2432.3.P3513 2015
271.00932—dc23 2015004512

For J.R.

Contents

Abbreviations

AP	*Sayings of the [Desert] Fathers* [*Apophthegmata Patrum*]:
	APalph — the Alphabetic Collection. See Introduction, n. 4.
	APanon — the Anonymous Collection. See Introduction, n. 5.
	APsys — the Systematic Collection. See Introduction, n. 6.
Bibliotheca	*Bibliotheca Hagiographica Graeca*
Butler	*The Lausiac History of Palladius*, ed. Cuthbert Butler, 2 vols. (Cambridge: Cambridge University Press, 1898, 1904).
Conf	John Cassian's *Conferences*
HE	*Ecclesiastical History*
Monks	*The History of the Monks in Egypt* [*Historia monachorum in Ægypto*]. See Introduction, n. 7.
OED	*Oxford English Dictionary*
PG	*Patrologia Graeca*
PS	*The Spiritual Meadow* [*Pratum Spirituale*]. See Introduction, n. 8.
SynaxCP	*Synaxarium Ecclesiae Constantinopolitanae*, ed. Hippolyte Delahaye, *Analecta Bollandiana* (Brussels, 1902).
Vita A	Athanasius's *Life of Antony* [*Vita Antonii*]. See Introduction, n. 2.

Translator's Introduction[1]

In the earlier part of the fourth century of this era, about the time Christianity became a legal religion in the Roman Empire, a considerable number of men and some women abandoned their usual places and ways of life to practice Christianity more intensely in remote locations. This change happened first in Egypt, and those who undertook it were the earliest Christian monks. Antony of Egypt (ca. 250–356) is frequently cited as the pioneer of that movement, although in Athanasius's *Life of Antony* (Vita A),[2] which largely contributed to that idea, Antony is said to have learned spiritual discipline (asceticism) from an earlier practitioner (Vita A 3.2–3). Antony's motivation and no doubt that of many others was a passage in the gospel where, after giving various directions, Jesus says to his followers, "But, if you want to be perfect [τέλειος], go sell your property, give [the proceeds] to the poor (you will have treasure in heaven), then come and follow me."[3] The surviving statistics must of course be treated cautiously, but it appears that a very substantial number of people heard and responded to this call, withdrawing either to share the life and teaching of a desert

[1] The translator wishes to express his sincere gratitude to his colleagues and mentors, Robert Jordan in Belfast and Rory Egan in Winnipeg, without whose generous cooperation this project might never have been realized.

[2] *Athanase d'Alexandrie, Vie d'Antoine*, ed. and trans. G. J. M. Bartelink, SCh 400 (Paris: Éditions du Cerf, 1994) (hereafter Vita A); *The Life of Antony: The Coptic Life and the Greek Life*, trans. Tim Vivian and A. N. Athanasakis, CS 202 (Kalamazoo, MI: Cistercian Publications, 2003).

[3] Vita A 2; Matt 19:2; see Matt 5:48: "Do you be perfect [τέλειοι] just as your heavenly father is perfect."

guru (*abba*, "elder") in Lower Egypt or to enroll in one of the more organized communities of the Thebaid.

A great deal of what is known about those early monks comes from one of two kinds of sources, both written in Greek. On the one hand, there are the so-called *Sayings of the Desert Fathers* (*Apophthegmata Patrum*), a somewhat misleading designation, for it covers not only sayings of but also tales about famous men and some women whose lives were devoted to spiritual discipline in the desert. Of the extant collections, the *Alphabetical*[4] and its supplement, the *Anonymous*,[5] were probably made a little before the year 500. Maybe a generation later, a selection from those collections was made. In this *Systematic Collection*[6] the material (supplemented by some sayings of Isaiah of Scete) is arranged under twenty-one heads representing the *desiderata* of the monastic profession, for example, 9. On Not Judging Persons, 10. On Discretion, 11. About Always Being on Watch, 12. On Praying "Without Ceasing."

One has continually to remind oneself when reading the *Apophthegmata* that their editors (possibly refugee monks in Palestine) were endeavoring to preserve in Greek an oral tradition in Coptic that had already been developing for a century

[4] *Apophthegmata patrum, collection alphabetica*, ed. Jean-Baptiste Cotelier, Monumenta Ecclesiae Graecae, t. 1 (Paris, 1647); reedited by J.-P. Migne, PG 65:71–440 (hereafter APalph); *Les Sentences des Pères du Désert: Collection alphabétique*, trans. Dom Lucien Regnault (Solesmes: Bellefontaine, 1966); *Give Me a Word: The Alphabetical Sayings of the Desert Fathers*, trans. John Wortley (Yonkers, NY: St Vladimir's Seminary Press, 2014).

[5] *Les Sentences des Pères du Désert, Série des Anonymes*, trans. Dom Lucien Regnault (Solesmes: Bellefontaine, 1985) (hereafter APanon); *The Anonymous Sayings of the Desert Fathers*, ed. and trans. John Wortley (Cambridge, UK: Cambridge University Press, 2013).

[6] *Les Apophtegmes des Pères: collection systématique*, ed. and trans. Jean-Claude Guy, 3 vols., SCh 387, 474, and 498 (Paris: Éditions du Cerf, 1993, 2003, 2005) (hereafter APsys); *The Book of the Elders: Sayings of the Desert Fathers; The Systematic Collection*, trans. John Wortley, CS 240 (Collegeville, MN: Cistercian Publications, 2012).

and a half in Egypt and elsewhere by their time. On the other hand, the travelogues (as we would call them today) are the direct memoirs of people who visited and even lived with the Desert Fathers. These may have been distorted in transmission, but they originate in precise Greek texts by specific authors. Of the three major examples, the earliest is *The History of the Monks in Egypt* (Monks).[7] In it are recorded the experiences of a group of seven monks from the Mount of Olives at Jerusalem who visited anchorites and monastic communities in the Thebaid and in lower Egypt during the winter of 394–395. On their return to Palestine one of their number (his name is not known) produced this report ca. 397. He tells how they undertook the arduous tour of Egypt in order to see for themselves the amazing way of life and accomplishments of the monks of whom they had heard so much. He does not minimize the great perils and dangers to which the visitors were exposed in the course of their journey (Monks, Epilogue), but he places particular emphasis on the disciplines the Egyptian monks endured and the wondrous works they were believed to perform. The avowed purpose of his book was to bring back to Palestine something "to inspire the emulation and recollection of advanced monks and for the building-up and benefit of beginners in the ascetic life" (Prologue 12).

The third and longest extant monastic travelogue is *The Spiritual Meadow* (*Pratum Spirituale*) of John Moschos,[8] who traveled the monastic world at the end of the sixth century and the

[7] *Historia Monachorum in Ægypto*, ed. André-Jean Festugière, *Subsidia Hagiographica* 53 (Brussels: Société des Bollandistes, 1971) (hereafter Monks); *Enquête sur les Moines d'Egypte*, trans. André-Jean Festugière, in *Les Moines d'Orient*, 4/1 (Paris: Les Éditions du Cerf, 1964); *The Lives of the Desert Fathers*, trans. Norman Russell (Oxford, UK, and Kalamazoo, MI: Mowbray/Cistercian Publications, 1981).

[8] John Moschos, *Pratum Spirituale*, ed. J.-P. Migne (after Fronto Ducaeus and J. -B. Cotelier), with the Latin translation of Ambrose Traversari, PG 87:2851–3112; *The Spiritual Meadow*, trans. John Wortley, CS 139 (Kalamazoo,

beginning of the seventh. Together with his friend (possibly his disciple: the relationship is not clear) Sophronios "the Sophist," the future patriarch of Jerusalem (633/4–648), he collected monastic data wherever he went "and worked them into a crown which I now offer to you [Sophronios], most faithful child, and through you to the world at large" (PS, Prologue). While the *Pratum Spirituale* is rich in anecdotal matter and a happy hunting ground for those who seek to discover how life was being lived at the end of the antique era, it portrays a monastic society now grown rather old, one in which the world and the desert are not nearly so sharply distinguished from each other as in the earlier documents.

By contrast, the remaining monastic travelogue, with which this volume is primarily concerned, preserves something of the youthful vigor and exuberance of monasticism in the early years of its existence, when the memory of Antony was still very much alive: the so-called *Lausiac History*, the work of Palladius.[9] This may have come to be known as a *history* by association with *The History of the Monks in Egypt*, but it is unlikely that Palladius had any knowledge of the earlier work. He certainly picked up some of the tales the Jerusalem monk had recorded, but he records them in different versions. On the other hand, Palladius undoubtedly knew the *Life of Antony* that Athanasius of Alexandria wrote sometime between 356, when Antony died, and his own death in 373, for he refers to it directly (8.6), and there are certain passages that might well have come directly from its pages (e.g., 21.16; see Vita A 66.3–6).

MI: Cistercian Publications, 1992); *Fioretti des moines d'orient*, trans. Christian Bouchet (Paris: Migne, 2006).

[9] Palladius of Hellenopolis / of Aspuna, *Historia Lausiaca*, ed. Cuthbert Butler, *The Lausiac History of Palladius*, 2 vols. (Cambridge, UK: Cambridge University Press, 1898, 1904); *Palladio, La Storia Lausiaca*, ed. G. J. M. Bartelink, trans. Marino Barchiesi (Milan: Fondazione Lorenza Valla and Libri Mondadori, 1974); *Les Moines du désert*, trans. Les sœurs carmelites de Mazille (Paris: Desclée de Brouwer, 1981).

Antony is mentioned far more often than any other person in the *Lausiac History* (about thirty-six times), and some of the most striking passages concern monks who cherished personal reminiscences of "the great one," as he was called (21.7, 8).

Of Palladius the man, we know not only the name but also a good deal else besides, because he did not hesitate to include a considerable amount of autobiographical material in his book, both physical and spiritual (see *Lausiac History* 23). Born in Galatia in the 360s, he enrolled as a monk on the Mount of Olives in his early twenties. He stayed there for about three years, during which time he encountered Rufinus of Aquileia and Melania the Elder. Possibly on their advice he left for Alexandria to learn the practice of Egyptian monasticism from a hermit named Dorotheos (2). He subsequently spent nine years living in the desert of Nitria and at The Cells, first with Macarius of Alexandria and then with Evagrius of Pontus, whose influence on him was very strong (38). In 399 Evagrius died, aged 53, and at about the same time Palladius fell ill. He says, "I fell sick with a sickness of the spleen and of the stomach. I was sent by the brothers from there to Alexandria after showing symptoms of dropsy. The physicians advised me to leave Alexandria for Palestine to take the air, for the air is light there and suitable for my condition" (35.11–12).

Arriving in Palestine, Palladius took up residence with Poseidon at Bethlehem; there he encountered Jerome (36). At some time he also lived with a famous hermit, Elpidius of Cappadocia, near Jericho (48.2). Then in 400 he was appointed to the Bythinian see of Hellenopolis by John Chrysostom, Patriarch of Constantinople since 398, whom he subsequently vigorously supported at the Synod of the Oak in 403. But faced with the hostility of the Augousta Eudoxia and accused of Origenism by Theophilus, the pope of Alexandria, Chrysostom was deposed and sent into exile.

Palladius then went to Rome to plead his case at the court of Innocent I (61.7), for which he was arrested when he returned to the capital. He was imprisoned for eleven months in a dark cell (35.13) and then sent into exile. For seven years he lived in the Thebaid, first at Syene (Aswân), then at Antinoë (or Antinoöpolis, now Shêkh 'Abâda). But with the accession of Theodosius II and his sister, the blessed Pulcheria, in 408, the opposition to John Chrysostom (who had died in exile the previous year) began to subside. In 413 Palladius was able to return to Galatia, where, in due course, he was appointed to the see of Aspuna. There he may have remained until his death, the date of which has not been established—possibly 425.

Palladius probably spent no more than twenty years as a monk before he became a bishop, and then only seven or eight years in exile in the Thebaid. No doubt this was sufficient time to gather the material for his book, but the number of his moves may seem inappropriate for one who had embraced the monastic calling.[10] There are numerous warnings about the dangers for monks of moving around, for example, "In the same way that a frequently transplanted tree is incapable of bearing fruit, so neither can a monk who moves from place to place accomplish virtue" (APanon 204 / APsys 7.43). Palladius's repeated changes of location may explain why he relates a great deal about the persons he encountered but not very much of their teaching; see, for example, the section on John of Lycopolis in *History of the Monks in Egypt*. And yet, unlike most other monastic writers, he occasionally inserts an injunction more appropriate to persons living in the world than to those under spiritual discipline, for example: "[The devil] contrives for us to travail for affluence under the pretense of caring for our relatives. . . . prompted by divine motivation, one can give relief

[10] He claims also to have "trod the streets of 106 cities and stayed for some time in most of them," maybe referring to monastic communities (*Lausiac History* 71.2 [see note]).

to one's relatives (if they are in need) without neglecting one's own soul. But when one tramples one's own soul under foot in caring for one's relatives, one falls foul of the law, counting the entire soul as worthless" (6.2–3).

Palladius lets it be known in various ways that he occupied no mean position in the social order. The elegance of his language alone suggests that claim to be true; of fourth- to sixth-century monastic writers, only his mentor Evagrius and Athanasius wrote Greek of similar sophistication. It is clear too that he habitually moved in exalted circles in the world, rubbing shoulders with persons of senatorial rank. His book has come to be known as *Lausiac* because he wrote it at the request of and dedicated it to one such person: Lausus, a eunuch in the imperial service.[11] He had been acquainted with Lausus since 391 (71.6); by the time Lausus received Palladius's book he had risen to the elevated position of chamberlain (*praepositus sacri cubiculi*) at Constantinople (420–422).

As Palladius well knew, this meant that Lausus was in an extremely advantageous position to influence their imperial majesties, Theodosius II and his sister, Pulcheria. When Lausus became chamberlain the emperor was not yet twenty; his sister, who was only two years older, had already more or less gathered the reins of power into her capable hands. Palladius makes no secret of the fact that he hopes to influence the sovereigns and the entire government through the minister: "May you be a guide for yourself, for those with you, for those under your authority, and for the most pious emperors, through whose good works all those who love Christ strive to be united with God" (Prologue 3). Thus Palladius's work is the only one of the major monastic writings not written for fellow monks to inspire them with models for their emulation but rather for

[11] "For it was not without the help of God that your mind was moved to charge me with the composition of this book and to commit to writing the lives of these holy ones" (71.5).

a man very much of the world, with the explicit intention of exerting *political* (albeit religious) influence. To what extent it contributed to the exemplary piety of the Augousta Pulcheria, who effectively ruled the Empire until her death in 453, we may never know.

Other features of the *Lausiac History* also distinguish it from most other monastic writings, such as Palladius's making the point that he intends to speak of both male and female ascetics: "In this book I must also commemorate some courageous women whom God granted equality in prizes with men so as not to allege that they are less vigorous in the quest for virtue" (41.1). Similarly he advises Lausus, "Seek the acquaintance of holy men and women" (Prologue 15). He gives both the elder and the younger Melania comprehensive treatment while according several other women honorable mention, including Piamoun (31), Olympia (56), the anonymous ascetic (60), and Magna (67). He also includes a surprisingly large number of references to monasteries for women (e.g., 1.4, 29–30, 33–34, 45.5, 49.2, and 70.3), not to mention his amazing statements that "There are twelve monasteries for women in that city of Antinoe" (59.1) and "In that city of Ancyra there are many other spinsters, about two thousand or more,[12] also some women distinguished by their continence and decency" (67.1).

Secondly, Palladius does not restrict himself to writing about shining models for emulation: "In order to praise those who lived well, I am not going to omit from the narrative those who have lived contemptuously [but will include them] as a warning to those who read it," he says (6.1). And after recounting the career of the indifferent Valens, he continues, "Just as among the sacred plants of Paradise there was the tree of the knowledge of good and evil, I have to include the lives

[12] Statistics, of which Palladius gives several (see 7.1–2, 8.6, 18.13, 20.1, 32.8–9, 56, 67.1), must of course be treated very cautiously.

of people like that in this little book for the security against stumbling of those who read it, so that if ever some success befalls them, they do not become high-minded on account of that virtue" (*Lausiac History* 25.6). There follow a series of bad examples of various kinds. One concludes that Palladius encountered not a few unpleasant characters in the course of his travels. ("I traveled . . . all over the Roman territory," he says [Prologue 5].) Among these was the great Jerome at Bethlehem, of whom he says, "he was so jealous that his jealousy obscured his literary skill" (36.6; see also 41.2).

Palladius concludes his work with a few words about "the brother who has been my companion from my youth until today" (71.1). As he never uses the first person plural when describing his travels, one concludes that he did not have a traveling companion in the way of John Moschos, who was accompanied by the future patriarch Sophronius two centuries later. It is now generally (but not universally) agreed that Palladius is referring to himself when he speaks of "the brother who has been my companion from my youth until today," as is Saint Paul in the passage from which the quotation a little further on is taken: "On behalf of such a one I will glory" (71.4; 2 Cor 12:5).

A Brief Note on the Text

The text of *Lausiac History* has an unusually complicated history because in the transmission process it became conflated and confused with other similar works. It was rescued at the end of the nineteenth century by the English Benedictine scholar, Dom Cuthbert Butler, who succeeded in isolating (inasmuch as is possible) the text that Palladius actually wrote. He also succeeded in disassociating the work from various doubts about its veracity, concluding, "The Lausiac History does not at all present the characteristics of a 'Gulliver's Travels' or of a romance. Quite the reverse: its chronology holds well together, its geography and topography are minutely accurate; its statements accord with well ascertained history and with the general conditions of the time. In other words, it is found to possess the ordinary marks of an authentic and veracious document."[1] Today few would dissent from this conclusion, largely confirmed by the more recent edition of G. J. M. Bartelink, on which the present translation is based and from whose copious footnotes I have drawn great benefit.

A highly respected scholar of our own day has pronounced the *Lausiac History* "the principal document for the history of Egyptian monasticism."[2] It appears to have enjoyed a similar reputation almost from when it was published, for, writing ca. 440, the ecclesiastical historian Socrates concluded a brief mention of some early Egyptian monks thus:

[1] Cuthbert Butler, *The Lausiac History of Palladius*, 2 vols. (Cambridge, UK: Cambridge University Press, 1898, 1904), 1:191.

[2] Henry Chadwick, *The Early Church* (London: Penguin, 1963), 191.

Should any one desire to become acquainted with their history, in reference both to their deeds and experiences and discourses for the edification of their auditors, as well as how wild beasts became subject to their authority, there is a specific treatise on the subject, composed by the monk Palladius, who was a disciple of Evagrius and gives all these particulars in minute detail. In that work he also mentions several women who practiced the same kind of austerities as the men referred to above.[3]

[3] Socrates, *Historia Ecclesiastica* 4.23, ed. G. C. Hansen, *Die Griechischen Christlichen Schriftsteller* (Berlin: Akademie Verlag, 1995).

Notes on Some Words

Abba, amma	father, mother
Accidie (*akêdia*)	"Sloth, torpor, especially as a condition leading to listlessness and want of interest in life" (OED), probably akin to depression
Apatheia	Literally "unfeeling"; indifference to physical conditions, a term largely associated with Evagrius, found rarely in the *Apophthegmata* but common in later monastic writing
Archimandrite	Literally "one in charge of a sheepfold." Here usually the superior of a monastery or (occasionally) a group of monasteries
Ascetic (*askêtês*)	One who practices *askêsis*
Askêsis	Literally a formation, usually meaning the practice of asceticism: the discipline associated with the monastic way of life, translated here as *spiritual discipline*
Coenobion (*koinobion*)	Literally "common life." A place or a community in which monks of either sex live together with shared worship, meals, and responsibilities. Sissinius (*Lausiac History* 49) may have had a monastery of men and women.
Hesychia (*hêsuchia*)	Not merely (or necessarily) silence (*siôpê*), but rather an interior silence characterized by a tranquil acquiescence in the will of God,

	producing a "profound calm and great peace within" (APsys 2.22)
Higoumen	The superior of a religious community
Lord-and-master	Translates *despotês*
Monastery	Any place where monks live, from the smallest hermitage to a vast coenobion of men or women; also called *askêterion* and *monê*
Porneia	All illicit sexual activity, mental and/or physical
Spinster	The word usually translated *virgin* (*parthenos*) is very confusing, because it has a variety of meanings in patristic Greek: *virgo intacta*, a young woman, a female monk (nun), a single woman of any age, a chaste person (of either sex), a religious widow, and so forth. As it is by no means always clear which meaning is intended, the word *spinster* has been resurrected to represent it. Sometimes the precise meaning can be discerned from the context, but not always.
Spiritual discipline	Translates *askêsis, q.v.*
Spiritual gift	Translates *charisma*
Virginity (*parthenia*)	E.g., "the yoke of virginity," *Lausiac History* 57.3; see *Spinster*

The Lausiac History

PROLOGUE

1. Since at various times many persons have left behind in life multiple and divers writings, some of them (inspired by grace given by God from above) for the edification and security of those who with faithful intent follow the precepts of the Savior, some (with corrosive intent) to please humans, having run riot to console those who crave for vainglory, and yet others out of some madness and agency of the demon who hates what is good, with conceit and delusion for the ruination of light-minded people and for the defilement of the spotless catholic church, have gained an entry into the thinking of the mindless in enmity for the holy way of life,

2. I too, lowly though I be, in deference to your greatness's stipulation, oh great lover of studies that enhance the mind, being now in my thirty-third year in the brothers' way of life (hence of the monastic profession), the twentieth year of my episcopate, and the fifty-sixth of my life, and being aware of your desire for tales of the fathers (both male and female), both those I have seen and those of whom I have heard, the ones with whom I lived, too, in the Egyptian desert, Libya, the Thebaid, Syene (where the ones called Tabennesiotes are), then in Mesopotamia, Palestine, and Syria and in the regions of the west, Rome, Campania, and

thereabouts, have decided to produce this book for you in narrative form and afresh,

3. that you might have a souvenir, sacred and beneficial to the soul, a perpetual medicine against forgetfulness and, by this dispelling all drowsiness arising from an irrational desire, every hesitation and meanness of spirit that arise in a character, sudden anger, agitation, grief, and irrational fear, and the distraction of the world, you may make progress in your chosen path of piety with unfading zeal. May you be a guide for yourself, for those with you, for those under your authority, and for the most pious emperors, through whose good works all those who love Christ strive to be united with God while you expect day by day the release of your soul, as it is written,

4. "It is good to experience release and to be with Christ,"* and "Prepare your work for departure and make it ready for the field."* The person who is ever mindful of death as something inevitable and imminent will not greatly sin; such a person will neither disregard the counsel of the teachings nor despise the crude and unlovely nature of the wording. For to express itself in a sophisticated manner is not the task of godly teaching but to sway the mind with representations of truth, as it is written, "Open your mouth with the word of God,"* and also, "Do not go astray from the interpretation of the elders, for they too learned from the fathers."*

*Phil 1:23

*Prov 24:27

*Prov 31:8

*Sir 8:9

5. Accordingly I, oh man of God, great lover of studies, in part following this text, have visited many of the holy ones, not just indulging an inquisitive notion, for I traveled for thirty days and even twice that, going on foot, walking in my

journey all over the Roman territory in God's name, gladly accepting the inconveniences of traveling for a meeting with someone who loved God in order to acquire that which I did not possess.

6. And if Paul, who so far exceeded me in his way of life, in knowledge, conscience, and faith, undertook the journey from Tarsus to Judaea to meet Peter, James, and John and spoke of it as though boasting, itemizing his own sufferings to stir up the reluctant and the lazy, saying, "I went up to Jerusalem to inquire of Cephas,"* was not satisfied with the report of Cephas's virtue but desired contact with him face to face, how much more then was I who owe ten thousand talents* obliged to do likewise, not for their benefit, but for my own?

*Gal 1:18

*Mark 18:24

7. They who wrote the lives of the fathers, Abraham and so forth—Moses, Elijah, and John—did not give their accounts to glorify them but for the benefit of those who read them.

As you are aware of these things, Lausus, most faithful servant of Christ, and set your own standards, be patient with our prating in protection of a pious mind that is tossed hither and thither by various forces seen and unseen and can be stilled only by unceasing prayer and the cultivation of one's personal spiritual life.

8. For many of the brothers, by giving themselves airs for their labors and almsgivings and boasting about their celibacy and virginity, gained confidence through meditation on the divine oracles and their zealous pursuits and failed to attain *apatheia*[1]

[1] A glossary to some of the words used in this text appears at the end of the introduction, pp. xxv–xxvi.

through lack of discretion, having fallen ill from certain meddling under the pretense of piety, whence arises officiousness and evil doing that distract from the doing of good deeds, which is the mother of the cultivation of one's personal spiritual life.

9. So, I beg of you, be courageous in not increasing your wealth, something that you have done in the past but then sufficiently diminished it by giving relief to those in need, and because of its service to virtue. Do not on an impulse or some irrational preconception fetter your resolution with an oath as a people-pleaser as some have done, in a competitive and audacious manner, enslaving their free will by the obligation of their oath not to eat or drink, only miserably through that oath to fall victim to the love of life, *accidie*, and delight, suffering the pains of perjury. If by reason you partake of something or by reason abstain from it, you will never sin.

10. For the reason behind our inner impulses is divine, excluding harmful elements and acquiring beneficial ones, for "the Law is not laid down for the righteous."* It is better to drink wine rationally than to drink water with conceit. Consider the holy men who drank wine rationally and the profane ones who drank water without reason; it is not the substance itself that is to be blamed or praised but the mind that is to be blessed or cursed, depending on whether it makes a good or a bad use of the substance. Joseph would drink wine with the Egyptians, but he was not damaged in his mind, because his judgment was firm.

*1 Tim 1:9

11. Pythagoras drank water, also Diogenes and Plato (the Manichees too and the rest of the band of

would-be philosophers), and they came to such a state of vainglory through intemperance that they denied God and worshiped idols. Those who accompanied the apostle Peter made use of wine, so that the Jews reviled the Savior, their teacher, for their partaking of it, saying, "Why do your disciples not fast as those of John do?"* And again, afflicting the disciples with reproaches, they said, "Your teacher is eating and drinking with publicans and sinners."* They would not have verbally attacked them in the case of bread and water, but clearly, their reference was to meat and wine.

*Mark 2:18

*Matt 9:11

12. The Savior too said to those who have an irrational admiration for water-drinking and who censure wine drinking, "John came on a path of righteousness* neither eating nor drinking," that is to say meat and wine, for he could not have lived without the other, "and they say, 'He has a demon.' The Son of Man came eating and drinking and they say, 'Behold a glutton and a tippler, a friend of publicans and sinners' on account of eating and drinking."*

*Matt 21:32

*Matt 11:18-19

So then, what are we to do? Let us go neither with those who blame nor with the ones who praise, but let us observe a reasonable fast with John, even if they say, "They have a demon." Or, if the body is in need of it, let us prudently partake of wine like Jesus, even if they say, "Here are gluttons and tipplers."

13. For in truth neither food nor abstaining from it is of any account, "but faith deployed in deeds through love."* When faith accompanies every deed, the one who eats and drinks stands uncondemned on account of faith, for "whatever is not

*Gal 5:6

Rom 14:23 through faith is sin." But since all of the offenders with a conscience corrupted by an irrational conviction will affirm that they partake (or do anything else) in faith, the Savior made a distinction, saying, "By their fruits you shall recognize them,"* and the godly apostle declares that the fruit of those who lead a life according to reason and conscience is "love, joy, peace, long-suffering, kindness, goodness, faithfulness, meekness, and temperance."*

*Matt 7:16

*Gal 5:22-23

14. Paul himself said, "The fruit of the spirit is" etc., etc., because the one who is seriously concerned to have those fruits will not eat meat or drink wine irrationally or aimlessly or inopportunely. Nor will such a one live with a bad conscience, for the same Paul also says, "Everyone fighting the good fight is temperate in all things."* When the body is healthy, a person avoids things that fatten; when it is sick or suffering or subject to grief or affliction, the person uses food and drink as medicine to ease the things that are causing grief. And one abstains from the things that damage the soul: wrath, envy, vainglory, *accidie*, backbiting, and irrational suspicion, while giving thanks to the Lord.

*1 Cor 9:25

15. Accordingly, having discussed that sufficiently, I am bringing another appeal to your love of learning. For all you are worth, flee from acquaintance with persons who offer no benefit and who adorn their skin incongruously, even if they are orthodox. Avoid heretics especially, for their hypocrisy is damaging, even though they seem to be dragging out their old age with their white hair and wrinkles. And even though you suffer no hurt from them on account of your noble behavior, you will become puffed up and conceited through

laughing at them, which is hurtful to you. Seek the acquaintance of holy men and women as through a window that admits light so that through them you may be able distinctly to perceive your own heart too (as in a neatly written book) and, by comparison with them, be able to assay your own slackness or lack of application.

16. The skin of the faces flourishing with their white hair and the wearing of their clothing, the lowly nature of their discourse, the piety of their words, and the grace of their thoughts—all this will empower you, even if you fall into *accidie*, for people's attire, their footstep, and the laughter of their teeth will report on them, as wisdom says.

Now that I am beginning the narratives, I will not leave those in cities, in villages, or in deserts unknown to you in my discourse. It is not, however, the place where they lived that is being looked for, but the nature of their endeavor.

1. ISIDORE

1. When I first trod the streets of Alexandria {in the second consulate of the great Emperor Theodosius,*[2] who is now among the angels for

*the second consulate of Theodosius I the Great, 370–395, occurred in 388

[2] In spite of textual scholars' labors, there are still some passages in the *Lausiac History* that are a little suspect, that is, that some scribe may have interpolated. These passages are indicated in the translation (as in G. J. M. Bartelink's edition) by being enclosed in curly brackets, thus: {. . .}. Words in square

his faith in Christ}, I encountered in the city a wondrous man endowed in every respect, both in morals and in knowledge: Isidore[3] the priest, the guestmaster of the Alexandrine church. He was said to have accomplished the first struggles of his youth in the desert; I saw his cell at the Mountain of Nitria.[4] He was an old man of seventy when I met him; he died in peace after living another fifteen years.

2. Until his death, Isidore never wore linen other than a headdress, never took a bath, and did not partake of meat. He had a body so constituted by grace that all those who did not know about his diet thought he lived in luxury. If I wanted to narrate the spiritual virtues of this man one by one, there would not be enough time. He was so charitably disposed and so peaceable that even his enemies, unbelievers though they were, revered his shadow on account of his great goodness.

3. He had such knowledge of the Holy Scriptures and of the divine beliefs that, even during the common meals of the brothers, he would go into an ecstasy and fall silent. When he was invited to explain his ecstasy he would say, "I wandered

---

brackets, thus [. . .], do not appear in the Greek text; they have been supplied to clarify the meaning.

[3] This is not Isidore "the Great" (Cassian, Conf 18.15), whose nine apophthegms are in APalph, but the Isidore who took refuge with John Chrysostom together with the four "Long Brothers" in 402 (Sozomen, HE 8.13) just before his death. Other persons of this name are mentioned by Palladius: a priest at Scete (*Lausiac History* 19.9) and a monk at Nitria who became a bishop (*Lausiac History* 46.2).

[4] The Valley of Nitria to the southwest of Alexandria extends for thirty miles and is six miles wide. It is enclosed by two mountain ranges, one of which is the Mountain of Nitria.

in my mind, rapt away by a vision." I was actually aware of this man's bursting into tears at table many times, and, on inquiring into the reason for the tears, I heard him saying, "I am ashamed to partake of the food of an irrational [beast] when I am rational and, by the power given to us by Christ, I ought to exist in a paradise of delight."

4. This man was known to the entire Senate at Rome and to the wives of the magnates from the time he first went there with Bishop Athanasius and afterward with Bishop Demetrius. Although he was affluent in wealth and in the abundance of his necessities, he did not write a will when he was dying. He did not leave one piece of gold or any property to his own sisters who were nuns; he committed them to Christ, saying, "He who created you will provide for your life, as he has for me." There was a community of seventy spinsters with his sisters.

5. When as a young man I visited him and besought him to instruct me in the monastic life, I being in the full flower of youth and not in need of words so much as of bodily toil, like a good colt-breaker he led me out of the city and took me to the place called Solitude, five miles away.

2. DOROTHEOS

1. He handed me over to Dorotheos,[5] a Theban ascetic who was passing his sixtieth year in a cave, and he told me to stay with him for three

[5] See Sozomen, HE 6.29.4. Other persons of this name are mentioned in *Lausiac History* 30, 58.2.

years to subdue the passions, for he was aware that the elder lived in great austerity. He enjoined me then to go back to him for spiritual teaching, but I fell ill and was unable to complete three years, so I came away from Dorotheos before three years were up, for his mode of life was austere and extremely severe.

2. All day long, in the burning heat of the desert, he collected stones along the sea coast and was always building with them, constructing cells that he would provide for those who were unable to build, completing one cell a year. When I once said to him, "What are you doing, father, killing your body in this great heat at your advanced age?" he said in reply, "It is killing me, I am killing it." He used to eat six ounces* of bread each day and a portion of chopped vegetables, drinking a proportionate amount of water. God is my witness: I was not aware of him stretching out his feet or sleeping on a mat or in a bed, for all night long he sat braiding rope from palm fronds to gain his living.

**unciae,* ca. 160 g.

3. Supposing that it was on my account that he was doing this, I made diligent inquiry and ascertained from some other disciples of his who were living alone that he had led this way of life from when he was young, that he never went to sleep on purpose and only shut his eyes when, working at something or eating, he was overcome by sleep, with the result that food often fell from his mouth at meal time through excessive drowsiness. Once when I was constraining him to lie down on a mat for a little, grieved to the heart, he said, "If you can persuade the angels to sleep, then you will also persuade the serious monk."

4. He once sent me to his well at about the ninth hour to fill the water jar for the shared meal at the ninth hour. Now it happened that, as I came there, I saw an asp down in the well. I drew the water no longer but went back and said to him, "We are done for, abba, for I saw an asp down in the well." He smiled graciously and looked at me for some time; then he shook his head and said, "If the devil takes it into his head to become a serpent down in every well or to fall as a tortoise into the water springs too, will you go on never drinking?" And going out he drew the water himself, and, fasting, he swallowed first, saying: "Where the cross visits no one's evil has any strength."

3. POTAMIAINÊ

1. This blessed Isidore met Antony*[6] of sacred memory, and he told me something he heard from him that is worth putting down in writing. In the time of Maximian the persecutor,* there was a most beautiful maiden called Potamiainê, somebody's handmaid. Although her master entreated her with many promises, he was not able to seduce her.

*Antony the Great, ca. 251–356

*probably not the emperor Maximian (286–310) but Maximinus II Daia (308–313), who renewed persecution of Christians

2. In the end he was so angry that he handed her over to the then-governor of Alexandria, betraying her as a Christian who was criticizing the times and the emperors for the persecutions. Her master bribed the governor, saying, "If she agrees to my proposition, keep her unpunished," but her master besought him, if she persisted in her

[6] There is no mention of this meeting in Vita A, but see Socrates, HE 4.25.

inflexibility, to torture her so she would not live to laugh his profligacy to scorn.

3. When she was brought before the judgment seat, her resolution was assaulted with various instruments of torture, including a large cauldron that the judge ordered to be filled with pitch and heated. When the pitch was boiling and thoroughly seething, he proposed to her, "Either go and submit to the wishes of your master or be quite sure that I shall order you to be put into the vessel." In answer she said to him, "May there never be such a judge as one who would order people to submit to profligacy!"

4. In a rage he ordered her to be thrown naked into the vessel, but she spoke out, saying, "By the head of your emperor whom you revere, if it is your decision to torture me like this, then order me to be let down into the vessel little by little so you might know with what great fortitude the Christ whom you do not know furnishes me." For an hour she was let down little by little; then she expired when the pitch reached her neck.

*ca. 313–398

4. DIDYMUS*

1. Very many men and women in the church of Alexandria were made perfect, worthy of the land of the meek.* Among them was the writer Didymus,[7] who was blind, with whom I had four meetings in ten years, coming to him from time

*see Matt 5:4; Ps 36:11

[7] Blind from infancy, Didymus became head of the Catechetical School at Alexandria; many writings are attributed to him.

to time; he died at the age of eighty-five. As he himself told me, he was blind, having lost his sight when he was four years old; he had neither learned to read nor studied with teachers.

2. For he had a vigorous natural teacher: his own mind, adorned with such grace of knowledge that what is written—"The Lord makes wise the blind"*—was literally fulfilled in him. He explained the Old and the New Testaments word by word.[8] He took such care with the teachings (minutely and securely setting out the meaning of them) that he surpassed all the old writers in knowledge.

*Ps 146:8

3. He once obliged me to offer a prayer in his cell, and I was unwilling to do so. He related how "The blessed Antony came into this cell three times to visit me. When he was asked by me to offer a prayer, he immediately knelt down in the cell and did not give me occasion to ask a second time, instructing me in obedience by deed. So if you are going to follow in the footsteps of his way of life, being a monk and embracing voluntary exile for virtue's sake, lay aside contention."

4. He told me this too: "I was pondering the life of Julian,* the wretched emperor and persecutor; one day when I was in anguish and had not touched a morsel of bread until late evening because of my concern, it came about that I was captured by sleep while sitting in my chair, and, in an ecstasy, I saw some white horses galloping with their riders, pronouncing, 'Tell Didymus

*Julian "the Apostate," 360–363

[8] Didymus is said to have memorized the entire Bible in addition to a considerable number of profane writings: Socrates, HE 4.25; Sozomen, HE 3.15.

that Julian died today at the seventh hour. Get up and eat and then send to Bishop Athanasius so he might know,' they said. I noted the time, the month, the week, and the day," he said, "and it was found to be so."

5. ALEXANDRA

1. He also told me about a maiden called Alexandra who abandoned the city and sequestered herself in a tomb, receiving the necessities of life through an aperture; for ten years she never looked a man or a woman in the face. Then in the tenth year she died, after laying herself out, with the result that she who habitually visited her, getting no answer, reported it to us. We unsealed the door, went in, and found that she had died.

2. The thrice-blessed Melania (of whom I shall later say more) said of her, "I did not look her in the face; I stood by the aperture and besought her to say why she had shut herself up in the tomb. She communicated with me through the aperture, saying, 'Somebody went out of his mind for me. So that I should not seem to distress him or to damage his reputation, I chose to take myself alive into the tomb rather than to give offense to a soul made in the image of God.' "

3. "I said to her," she said, " 'How can you stand it, not speaking to anybody and struggling against *accidie*?' She said, 'I pray every hour from dawn to the ninth hour while spinning linen; the remaining hours I go over the holy patriarchs, prophets, apostles, and martyrs in my mind; then, when I have eaten my bread, I pass the remain-

ing hours in perseverance, awaiting my end with gentle hope.'"

6. THE RICH SPINSTER

1. In order to praise those who lived well, I am not going to omit from the narrative those who have lived contemptuously [but will include them] as a warning to those who read it. There was a spinster in Alexandria who was humble in appearance but haughty in temperament. She was very wealthy but did not give anything away to a stranger, a spinster, a church, or a pauper. Many exhortations of the fathers notwithstanding, she would not wean herself off material possessions.

2. She had relations, and, of these, she adopted her own sister's daughter, night and day promising her estate, for she had fallen away from a desire for heaven. This too is a form of the devil's misleading: he contrives for us to travail for affluence under the pretense of caring for our relatives. He admits that he does not care about family, advocating the killing of brother, mother, and father.

3. And even if he seems to put it to us to care for our relatives, he does not do it out of kindness to them but to give the soul practice in injustice, for he knows the statement, "The unjust shall not inherit the kingdom of God."* But, prompted by divine motivation, one can give relief to one's relatives (if they are in need) without neglecting one's own soul. But when one tramples one's own soul under foot in caring for one's relatives, one falls foul of the law, counting the entire soul as worthless.

*1 Cor 6:9

4. The sacred psalmist sings of those who take care of their souls in fear, "Who shall ascend to the
Ps 23:3-4 mountain of the Lord?" (it being implied: very few). "Or who shall stand in his holy place? He that has clean hands and a pure heart; who has not lifted up his soul unto vanity." They who "lift it up unto vanity" are all those who do not care about the virtues, thinking that [the soul] is dissipated together with the body.

5. The most blessed Macarius[9] wanted to do what they call a bloodletting on this spinster to alleviate her desire for affluence. He was a priest and the warden of the poorhouse for lepers; he devised a stratagem like this: as a young man he had worked with precious stones as what they call a gem engraver. He went and said to her: "Some precious stones have come into my hands, emeralds and aquamarines; I cannot say whether they were found or stolen. They are not being submitted for valuation because they are beyond price. He who possesses them is selling them for five hundred pieces of gold.

6. "If you are thinking of taking them you could recover your five hundred gold pieces with one stone, then use the rest of them to adorn your niece." The spinster was hooked and caught; she fell at his feet saying, "By your feet let nobody else take them." So he urged her, "Get yourself to my house and take a look at them," but she could not wait. She threw him the five hundred pieces of gold, saying, "As

[9] This is neither of the two famous Macarii; he is mentioned by Cassian, Conf 14.4: "a man of extraordinary gentleness and patience."

you will; take them, for I do not want to see the man who is selling."

7. [Macarius] took the five hundred pieces of gold and handed them over for the needs of the poorhouse. Time went galloping by, but since the man seemed to have a great reputation in Alexandria for his love of God and his compassion (he flourished into his hundredth year, and we ourselves spent some time with him), she hesitated to remind him. Finally she found him in church and said to him, "I pray you, what do you bid me do about those stones for which we gave the five hundred pieces of gold?"

8. In answer he said to her, "The moment you gave me the gold I paid it down on the price of the stones, and if you want to come and see them at the hospice (for that is where they are), come and see if they please you; otherwise, take your gold." She came most gladly. The poorhouse had women on the upper floor, men on the ground floor. He brought her to the gate and said to her, "Which do you want to see first, the aquamarines or the emeralds?" "As you please," she said to him.

9. Leading her to the upper story, he showed her women missing limbs and with disfigured faces, saying to her, "here are my aquamarines." Then he led her back down and showed her the men. "Here are the emeralds," he said to her; "if they please you; otherwise, take your gold." That woman went out confounded, and when she came away, she fell ill from her great sorrow that she had not done the deed in a godly fashion. She thanked the priest later on; the girl of whom she had taken charge married, then died childless.

7. THOSE AT NITRIA

1. When I had been staying at the monasteries around Alexandria for three years and had encountered about two thousand excellent and very zealous men, I went away from there and came to the Mountain of Nitria.[10] There is a lake situated between this mountain and Alexandria; it is called Mareotis, and it is seventy miles long. Sailing along it for a day and a half I came to the Mountain on its southern side.

2. Situated alongside the Mountain is the great desert that extends to Ethiopia, to the land of the Maziks, and to Mauritania. There are about five thousand men living on this Mountain, following various ways of life, each one according to his ability and wishes, so it is possible for them to live alone or in pairs or together in large numbers.

[10] "We also went down to Nitria where we saw many great anchorites, some natives, some foreigners, outreaching each other in virtue, engaged in rivalry with respect to spiritual discipline, manifesting all virtue and striving to outdo each other in their way of life. Some were devoting themselves to contemplation, some to practical measures. For when some of them saw us coming from afar across the desert they came to meet us with water; some washed our feet, some cleaned our clothes, some invited us to eat, some to learn about virtue, some to the contemplation and knowledge of God. . . . They inhabit a desert region, and their cells are some distance apart so that no one can recognize another or hear [his] voice. They live in profound *hêsychia,* each one shut up on his own. Only on Saturday and Sunday do they congregate in the churches and meet with each other. . . . They are so far distant from each other that some of them come three or four miles to the *synaxis,* and yet they have such great love for each other and for the brotherhood. As many often come wanting to be saved with them, each one hastens to offer his own cell for their accommodation" (Monks 20, 5–8).

There are seven bakeries on this Mountain serving both those who are there and also the anchorites out in the desert: six hundred men.

3. I stayed on that Mountain for a year and reaped great benefit from the blessed fathers Asision the great, Poutoubastos, Asiônos, Kronios, and Serapion. Then, spurred on by them with many stories of other fathers, I entered the inner desert. On that Mountain of Nitria there is a great church at which three palm trees stand, each with a whip hanging from it: one for monks who are at fault, one for robbers if they attack, one for casual visitors. Thus all those who are at fault and are convicted as being worthy of stripes receive the said [punishment] on the back while embracing the palm tree; then they are set free.

4. There is a guesthouse situated adjacent to the church where they welcome a stranger who comes that way all the time he is there (even if he stays two or three years)—until he leaves of his own free will. For one week they permit him to do nothing, but they divert him with tasks on subsequent days: either in the garden, in the bakery, or in the kitchen. If it is a person of distinction, they give him a book, but they do not allow him to have contact with anybody until a certain hour. There are also physicians living on this Mountain and also pastry cooks. They drink wine, and there is wine for sale.

5. All these men work with their hands in the manufacture of linen so that they are all self-sufficient. About the ninth hour it is possible to stand and hear how the sound of psalm singing is coming out of each monastery, so that one feels as though one were raised up into Paradise. They only come

to church on Saturday and Sunday. There are eight leading priests at this church, and, as long as the first priest is living, none other presides, preaches, or passes judgment in it: they only sit quietly before him.

6. This Arsisios and many other elders with him (whom we saw) were contemporaries of the blessed Antony. Some of them even claimed to have seen Amoun of Nitria, whose soul Antony saw being taken up, conducted by angels.* Arsisios said that he also saw Pachomius of Tabennesi, a man who was a prophet and the archimandrite of three thousand men—of whom I shall speak later on.[11]

*Vita A 60.1–3

8. AMOUN OF NITRIA

1. Arsisios used to say that Amoun lived like this: he was an orphan, and as a young man of twenty-two he was obliged by his uncle to be married to a woman. As he was unable to resist his uncle's coercion, he allowed himself to be married and installed in the bridal chamber, submitting to all the conventions of marriage. When everybody had left after settling them in the bridal chamber and in bed, up got Amoun, locked the door, sat down, and called to his blessed partner, saying to her,

2. "Come, my lady; then I will explain the situation to you: the wedding by which we were married is this and has no more to it. We shall do well if henceforth each one of us sleeps alone, so that we may please God by keeping virginity intact."

[11] See *Lausiac History* 32; three thousand is also the number given in Monks 3.1.

Taking a small book out of his bosom he read to the maiden (who had no knowledge of the Scriptures) in the guise of the apostle and of the Savior. For the most part adding everything from his own mind, he presented the argument for virginity and purity. The result was that she was convinced by the grace of God and said,

3. "I too am convinced, sir; what do you bid then?" "I bid each of us to remain alone from now on," he said, and she did not object. "Let us live in the same house," she said, "but in separate beds." So for eighteen years he lived in the same house with her, spending all day in the garden and in the balsam patch, for he was a balsam grower. (Balsam grows like a vine; it requires a lot of work, having to be tended and pruned.) In the evening he would come in, offer prayers, and eat with her. Then again, after offering the nighttime prayer, out he would go.

4. When they had lived like that for some time and both of them had attained *apatheia*, Amoun's prayers were effective, and she finally said to him, "I have something to say to you, my lord, so that if you hear me, I may be convinced that you love me in a godly manner." "Say what you wish," he said to her, and she said to him, "It is right and proper that we should live apart, since you are a man who is cultivating righteousness, and I am she who has zealously pursued the same path as you. But it is inappropriate for such virtue on your part to be hidden, living with me in chastity."

5. Giving thanks to God, he said to her, "So you have this house and I will build myself another house?" Out he went and came to the inner part

of the Mountain of Nitria (for at that time there were not yet any monasteries there), and he built himself a cell consisting of two domed chambers. He lived in the desert another twenty-two years and then died, or rather fell asleep. He used to see his blessed partner twice a year.

6. The blessed Bishop Athanasius related this wonder in *The Life of Antony*: [Amoun] came to the River Lykos with Theodore, his disciple. Hesitating to take his clothes off lest Theodore see him naked, he found himself on the other side without a ferry, transported by an angel.* This Amoun so lived and so died that the blessed Antony beheld his soul being taken up by angels.* I myself crossed that river in a ferry with trepidation; it is a branch of the great Nile.

*Vita A 60.5–9

*Vita A 60.1–4

9. ÔR

There was a man practicing asceticism at this Mountain of Nitria whose name was Ôr; the entire brotherhood used to bear witness to his virtue, especially that godly person Melania, who came to the Mountain before me, for I never came across him while he was alive. They used to tell this of him in the narratives, that he did not speak falsely, did not swear, did not curse anybody, and did not speak without the need to do so.*

*see APalph, Ôr 2

10. PAMBÔ

1. Also of this Mountain was the blessed Pambô, the teacher of Bishop Dioscorus, Ammônios, the

brothers Eusebius and Euthymius and Origen, and the nephew of that wondrous man Dracontius. This Pambô had acquired a wealth of virtuous deeds and made significant progress; for example, he had great disdain for silver and gold, as the word [of the Lord] requires.

2. The blessed Melania recounted to me, "When I first came to Alexandria from Rome and heard about the virtue of this man, it was the blessed Isidore who told me and led me to him in the desert. I brought him a chest containing three hundred pounds of silver, inviting him to share my wealth. But he just sat there, braiding fronds, and only blessed me with his voice, saying, 'May God reward you.'

3. "And he said to Origen, his steward, 'Take this and use it for the advantage of the entire brotherhood in Libya and the islands, for those monasteries are in greater need.' He instructed him not to give to any [monastery] in Egypt, for that country was more prosperous. I stood there (she said), expecting to be honored and glorified by him for the gift, and when I heard nothing from him, I said to him, 'I want you to know, Sir, how much there is: three hundred pounds.'

4. "Without even looking up at all, he answered me, 'He to whom you brought them has no need of a weighing machine. He who weighs out the mountains knows much better how much silver there is. If it was to me that you gave it, you did well to speak up, but if it was to God who did not despise the two mites,* keep quiet.' That was how the Lord dealt with me when I came to the Mountain," she said.

*Mark 12:42; Luke 21:2

5. "The man of God died a little later; he had neither a fever nor an illness but was stitching up a basket. He was seventy years old. He summoned me, and, putting in the last stitch to complete the work, at the point of death he said to me, 'Receive this basket from my hands and remember me; I have nothing else to leave you.' I prepared him for the tomb, wrapped the body in linen, and buried it." With that she went away from the desert and kept the basket with her until she died.

6. When this Pambô was dying, he is alleged to have said to those who were present, to the renowned Origen the priest and steward, and to Ammônios, and to the rest of the brothers at the moment of departing, "From the time when I came to this place in the desert, built my cell, and took up residence in it, I have no recollection of eating bread that was given to me: only what my hands produced. I have not regretted a word I have spoken until this very moment, and so off I go to God, without even having begun to serve him."

7. Origen and Ammônios also bore witness to him, telling us, "When he was asked about a phrase in Scripture or some other matter, he would never answer immediately, but would say, 'I have not found it yet.' Three months even went by without his giving an answer, saying he had not reached it. Yet folk received his replies as though from God, and these came to be treated with circumspection like divine precepts." There was one virtue in which he was said to surpass everyone else, including Antony the Great: accuracy in speech.

8. An event of this kind is reported of Pambô: Piôr the ascetic visited him, and he brought his own

bread. He was reproved by Pambô, "For what reason have you done this?" "In order not to inconvenience you," the other replied. Pambô taught him a lesson by letting the silence speak. Sometime later Pambô went to visit Piôr, having dampened the bread he was bringing. Then, when he was asked, he said, "I even dampened it so as not to inconvenience you."

11. AMMÔNIOS

1. This Ammônios (Pambô's disciple) together with {three other brothers and} his two sisters, excelling in love for God, went to live in the desert, the women making themselves a dwelling and he one for himself, a sufficient distance apart from each other. As the man was an outstanding scholar, a certain city desired him to be bishop. They went to the blessed Timothy,* beseeching him to ordain him to be their bishop.

*presumably the Patriarch of Alexandria Timothy I, 380–384

2. "Bring him to me," he said, "and I will ordain him." When they came [to Ammônios] with a retinue and he saw that he was caught, he besought them, swearing that he would not accept ordination, and neither would he come out of the desert, but they would have none of it. With them looking on, he took a pair of scissors and sheared off his left ear at the base and said to them, "From now on be assured that it is impossible for me to become [a bishop] since the law forbids a person with an ear cut off to be brought into the priesthood."

3. With that they left him and went away. They came and told the bishop, and he said to them, "Let that law be observed by the Jews; even if

you brought me somebody with his nose cut off, I would ordain him if he had a worthy character." Off they went again and besought him, but he swore to them, "I will cut out my tongue if you coerce me," so they left him and went away.

4. This amazing thing is told of this Ammônios: he never spared himself when delight in his flesh rose up to attack him. He would apply a red-hot iron to his members, with the result that he was always scarred. From when he was a young man until death his fare at table was raw, for he never ate anything that had been cooked except bread. He had memorized the Old and New Testaments, and among the writings of learned men (Origen, Didymus, Pierios, and Stephen) he had read six million* as the fathers of the desert bear him witness.

*lines?

5. He was a consolation like none other to the brothers in the desert. {The blessed Evagrius, that spiritual and discerning man, used to give this judgment on him, saying, "I never saw a person more advanced in *apatheia* than he was.} {He was once in Constantinople for some necessity . . . and died a little later. He was buried in the martyrium called Rufinian, and his tomb is said to cure all those who have a fever.}

12. BENJAMIN

1. A man called Benjamin lived an utterly ascetic life on this Mountain of Nitria for eighteen years and then was found worthy of the spiritual gift of healings. Everyone on whom he laid a hand or to whom he gave oil he had blessed was relieved of all illness. This man who was found

worthy of such a grace was afflicted with dropsy eight months before his death; his body swelled up to such an extent that he looked like another Job. When Bishop Dioscorus, priest of the Mountain of Nitria at that time, visited the blessed Evagrius and me, he said to us,

2. "Come and see a new Job, who, with his body so swollen up and an incurable disease, possesses boundless thanksgiving." So we went and saw somebody whose body was so swollen that a finger of his hand was not able to grasp the other fingers. We were unable to contemplate the terribleness of his suffering and turned our eyes away. Then that blessed Benjamin said to us, "Pray, my sons, that my inner man not be afflicted with dropsy, for this [outer man] neither benefited me when I was well nor harmed me when I was sick."

3. For eight months an exceedingly wide litter was set out for him, on which he sat all the time, unable to lie down in a bed on account of the remaining necessities, and, though being in this suffering, he was healing others. We have felt compelled to relate this suffering so that we be not dismayed when some such circumstance befall the righteous. When he died the jambs and pillars of the door were removed so that his body could be carried out of the house, so great was his swelling.

13. APOLLONIUS

1. One Apollonius by name, a former merchant, renounced the world and took up residence at the Mountain of Nitria. Having been unable to learn a trade or the practice of writing (for he had

grown old) during the twenty years he lived at the Mountain, he purchased in Alexandria all kinds of medicines and supplies with his own resources, and by his own efforts he used to relieve the entire brotherhood in cases of sickness.

2. He was to be seen going around the monasteries from dawn until the ninth hour, passing from door to door to see whether anybody lay sick. He would be carrying raisins, pomegranates, eggs, wheat bread—the sort of things sick people need. Such was the way of life he found beneficial for him in his old age. When he was dying, he bequeathed his odds and ends to a person like himself, begging him to fulfil the same ministry. As there were five thousand monks living at the Mountain, there was need of this visitation, too, for the place was desert.

14. PAÊSIOS AND ISAIAH

1. There were also the brothers Paêsios and Isaiah, whose father was the merchant Spanodromos. After he died they divided among themselves what they possessed in real estate, five thousand pieces of gold, and what there was of clothing and slaves. They consulted each other and counseled themselves, saying, "What style of life are we to take up, brother? If we engage in the commerce our father followed, we too are going to leave the fruits of our labor to others;

2. "also, perhaps we will fall prey to robbers or the sea. Come then, let us embark on the monastic life so we may both profit from our father's estate and not lose our souls." So the aim of the monastic

life pleased them, but they were found to be of different minds. Having divided the money, each one held fast to the aim of pleasing God, but with an alternative way of life.

3. One of them gave away all he had to monasteries, churches, and prisons. Having learned a lowly trade to provide himself with bread, he devoted himself to spiritual discipline and prayer. The other one gave nothing away but built himself a monastery, and, associating himself with a few brothers, he took in every stranger, every sick person, every old person, and every pauper; on Saturdays and Sundays he provided three {or four} sittings. That is how he spent his money.

4. After they had both died there were different opinions concerning their blessedness, as both of them had attained perfection. This one was pleasing to some, that one to others. As strife broke out in the brotherhood with regard to their good reputations, they went to the blessed Pambô and, expecting to learn which was the greater way of life, assigned the distinction to him. But he told them, "Both are perfect: the one demonstrated the work of Abraham, the other of Elijah."

5. So they said to him, "By your feet, how is it possible for them to be equal?" They who esteemed the ascetic more highly said, "He performed an evangelical work, for he sold everything and gave to the poor; hour by hour, by day and by night he was carrying the cross and following the Savior also in prayers." But those who strove against them said, "This [other] showed so much to those in need that he even seated himself on the highways and gathered up the afflicted; he gave repose not only

to his own soul but also to many others, caring for the sick and succoring them."

6. Said the blessed Pambô to them, "I tell you again: both are equal. I assure each one of you that even if the one were not so advanced in spiritual discipline he would not have become worthy to be compared with the other's goodness, for, in giving repose to strangers, that one gained repose for himself together with them, and if he seemed to be weighed down by the toil, he gained repose on account of it. But wait so that I might receive a revelation from God; coming after that you will find out." So they came a few days later and besought him again and, as though he were in the presence of God, he said to them: "I saw them both standing together in Paradise."

15. MACARIUS THE YOUNGER

1. While herding flocks, a young man named Macarius, eighteen years old, accidentally committed a murder while playing with persons of his own age on the shores of Lake Mareotis. He went into the desert without saying a word to anybody and advanced to such fear of God and man that he lost all physical sensation; he stayed outdoors in the desert for three years. The land is arid in those parts, and everybody knows it, some by hearsay, some by experience.

2. Later on he built himself a cell, and when he had lived in his cell another twenty-five years he was found worthy of the spiritual gift of spitting on demons by delighting in the solitude. Having spent considerable time with him, I asked him how his

conscience felt about the sin of murder. He said he was so far distant from grieving that he was even thankful for the murder, for the accidental murder had become the occasion of salvation for him.

3. He said this calling the Scriptures to witness that Moses would not have been deigned worthy of the divine vision {or of such a gift or of the authorship of the holy words} if he had not taken refuge in the Mountain of Sinai for fear of Pharaoh on account of the murder he had committed in Egypt. I do not say this to point the way to murder but showing that there are circumstantial virtues when one is not willingly advancing to the good. Some virtues are freely chosen, some circumstantial.

16. NATHANAEL

1. There was another of the old-timers named Nathanael. I did not catch up with him when he was alive, for he had died fifteen years before my arrival, but when I encountered his fellow ascetics and contemporaries I was inquisitive about the man's virtue. They showed me his cell, in which nobody was living anymore because it was quite near to habitation. He built it at a time when anchorites were very few. They recounted this especially of him: he had such patient endurance in his cell that he was never shaken in his determination.

2. For example, when he was first led astray by the demon who leads astray and deceives everybody, he thought that he was falling into *accidie* because of the first cell, so he went and built another one, nearer to the village. But three or four months after he had finished the cell and was living in

it, the demon came by night, carrying an ox hide whip as torturers do and in the form of a soldier dressed in rags, cracking his whip. The blessed Nathanael spoke to him, saying, "Who are you, acting like that in my guestroom?" "I am he who drove you out of that cell," the demon replied, "and so I have come to send you packing from this one."

3. Aware now that he had been deceived, Nathanael returned again to the first cell, and passing thirty-seven years [there] he did not step beyond the door, striving contentiously against the demon, who, endeavoring to force him to leave, showed him things more numerous than one can possibly describe. Here is another example: watching out for a visit of seven holy bishops that took place through either the providence of God or temptations, the demon almost diverted Nathanael from his determination. After offering a prayer, the bishops were coming out, but he did not bring them on their way, not even a footstep.

4. The deacons said to him, "This is pride, abba, not bringing the bishops on their way," but he said to them, "I am dead both to my lords the bishops and to the whole world. I have a secret purpose, and God knows my heart; so I am not bringing them on their way." Missing the point of this business, nine months before Nathanael's death the demon took on an appearance: he became as a ten-year-old child leading an ass with some loaves in a basket. Being near to Nathanael's cell in the late evening, he made as if the ass had fallen and the child was crying,

5. "Abba Nathanael, have mercy on me and give me a hand." Hearing the voice of the pre-

tended child, Nathanael opened the door a little and, standing inside, said to him, "Who are you, and what do you want me to do for you?" "I am so-and-so's lad, and I am bringing loaves; there is to be an *agape* for such-and-such a brother, and tomorrow morning, Saturday, they will need loaves for the offering. I beg of you not to abandon me lest I be eaten by hyenas." (There were many hyenas in those parts.) The blessed Nathanael stood speechless and became very dizzy. Disturbed in his inner self, he thought to himself, "I am going to fall short either of the commandment or of my own purpose."

6. But later he came to the conclusion that it was better not to be detached from his purpose of so many years, to put the devil to shame. When he had prayed, he said to the child who was speaking, "Listen, child: if you are in need, I have faith in the God whom I serve that he will send you aid and that neither hyenas nor anything else will do you any harm. But if you are a temptation, God will reveal the falsehood henceforth." He shut the door and went in. Put to shame at this reverse, the demon was transformed into a whirlwind and into wild asses, bounding and noisily running off. Such was the struggle of the blessed Nathanael; such was his way of life, and so he concluded it.

17. MACARIUS THE EGYPTIAN*

*the Great

1. Of those unforgettable two men named Macarius there is a great deal that is hard to believe; I hesitate to say or to write it for fear of acquiring the reputation of being a liar. The Holy Spirit has

revealed that "The Lord destroys all those who speak falsehood,"* so believe me who am not lying, and be not unbelieving. One of these men named Macarius was an Egyptian by race, the other a citizen of Alexandria, a dried-fruit merchant.

*Ps 5:7

2. First I will tell of the Egyptian,[12] who lived a total of ninety years, spending sixty of them in the desert, where he went as a young man of thirty. He was thought worthy of such discretion that he was called "young elder"; on that account he made rapid progress. By the time he was forty he received grace in respect of spirits, both of cures and foretelling the future; he was also deemed worthy of the priesthood.

3. There were two disciples with him in the innermost desert, at a place called Scete. One of them was an attendant at his side [to deal with] those who came to be healed, while the other spent his time in a cell very close by. When some time had gone by, having had resort to the second sight, he said to him who attended him (his name was John, and he subsequently became priest, occupying the place of Macarius himself), "Listen to me, brother John, and hold fast to my admonition. You are being tempted, and it is the spirit of avarice that is tempting you.

[12] Born ca. 300, Macarius was a Coptic peasant, a camel driver dealing in niter. In the 330s he founded Scete, where he died ca. 390. He met Antony at least once. Farther to the west than either Nitria or the Cells, Scete (or Scetis, Wadi El Natrun, about sixty miles from Alexandria) became the most famous of the monastic centers of Egypt but was three times devastated by the Mazics at the beginning of the fifth century.

4. "I have seen that it is so, and I know that, if you will patiently bear with me, you will be made perfect in this place and glorified and 'the scourge will not come near your dwelling.'* But if you disobey me, you will end up like Gehazi, as you are sick with his illness."* In the event, he disobeyed after the death of Macarius (another fifteen or twenty years later), and he suffered such elephantiasis for having depleted [goods intended for] the poor that you could not find an untouched place on his body on which to place a finger; that is what the holy Macarius had prophesied.

*Ps 90:10

*2 Kgs 5:20-27

5. It would be superfluous to tell of food and drink since there is no gluttony or indifference to be found even among the less strict in those parts, on account both of the scarcity of the necessities of life and also of the zeal of the inhabitants. But I will speak of the rest of his spiritual discipline. They used to say that he was in an unending ecstasy and that he spent more time involved with God than with the things beneath heaven. The following wonders are reported of him:

6. An Egyptian man was in love with a respectable married woman, and since he was unable to seduce her, he spoke to a magician, saying, "Get her to love me or do something so that her husband throws her out." Well paid, the magician used tricks of wizardry to make her look like a mare. The husband was dumbfounded when he came in and saw a mare lying in his bed. The man wept, he lamented; he spoke to the beast but received no reply. He sent for the village priests,

7. brought them in, and showed them; he could not grasp the matter. For three days she partook

neither of hay like a mare nor of bread like a human, depriving herself of both foods. Finally, in order that God should be glorified and the virtue of the holy Macarius be displayed, it came into her husband's heart to take her into the desert. He put a halter on her like a horse and led her into the desert. The brothers were standing near to Macarius's cell when the couple drew near, and they reproved her husband, saying,

8. "Why did you bring that mare here?" He said to them, "For her to receive mercy." They said to him, "What is wrong with her?" to which the husband answered them, "She was my wife and was turned into a horse; this is the third day she has not eaten anything." The brothers brought the couple to the holy one who was inside, praying—for God had revealed the matter to him, and he was praying for her. In replying to the brothers, the holy Macarius said, "You are horses yourselves and people with horses' eyes;

9. "that is a woman, not transformed at all—except in the eyes of those who have been deceived." He blessed some water, poured it on her naked [body] from the top of her head, and prayed; immediately he made her appear as a woman to them all. He gave her food and obliged her to eat. He dismissed her together with her husband, she giving thanks to the Lord. He admonished her, saying, "Never again be separated from the church; {never again stay away from communion}. These things happened to you because for five weeks you have not attended the mysteries."[13]

[13] See Monks 20.17 for another version of this story.

10. Here is another deed of Macarius's spiritual discipline. Over a long time he dug a subterranean passage from his cell half a furlong in length* and made a grotto at the end of it. Whenever many people were assailing him, he would secretly leave his cell and go away to the grotto, and nobody would find him. One of his advanced disciples was telling [us this], and he said that when Macarius was going off to the grotto he used to offer twenty-four prayers and twenty-four coming back.

*about a hundred meters

11. The rumor did the rounds that, in order to persuade a heretic who did not agree that there is a resurrection of bodies, Macarius raised up a dead person, and that rumor persisted in the desert. A young man possessed of a demon and bound to two other young men was once brought to Macarius by his mother, she in tears. This is what the operation of the demon was: after the young man had eaten three *modii* of bread and drunk a κιλικίσιον of water,[14] he would bring up the provisions as steam by belching; thus meat and drink were dissipated as though by fire.

12. There is in fact a type [of demon] called "fiery." There are different types of demons just as there are of humans, different not in substance but in mentality. Now this young man would eat his own excrement when he was not being supervised by his mother, and he often drank his own urine. As the mother was weeping and imploring the holy one, he took the young man and prayed for him, interceding with God. When the condition

[14] Roughly twenty-five liters of bread [!] and an uncertain amount of water.

abated after a day or two, the holy Macarius said to her,

13. "How much do you want him to eat?" In reply she said, "Ten pounds of bread." He reproved her because it was a great deal; having prayed for him with fasting, in seven days he stopped him at three pounds, obliging him to work too, and when he had cured him in that way he restored him to his mother. God worked that wonder through Macarius. I never came across him, for he had died a year before I came into the desert.

*the city dweller

18. MACARIUS OF ALEXANDRIA*

*ca. 293–393

1. But I did come across the other Macarius, the Alexandrine;* he was priest at what they call The Cells. I stayed nine years at The Cells, and he was still alive during my first three years there. Some of the things I witnessed, some I heard from him, and some I learned from others. This then was his spiritual discipline: if ever he heard of some practice he certainly embraced it. When he heard from some people that the folk at Tabennesi ate nothing cooked throughout Lent, he resolved not to eat anything treated with fire for seven years, and, apart from raw cabbage (if there was any) and steeped lentils, he ate nothing.

*the meaning of this word is uncertain

2. When he had established this virtuous behavior, he heard of yet another person who ate a pound of bread. He broke his own biscuit,* put the fragments into vessels, and resolved to eat as much as the hand could lift out. He recounted with a smile, "I laid hold of many pieces but could not lift them all out on account of the narrowness of

the opening; like a tax collector it would not let me do so." He maintained that spiritual discipline for three years, eating four or five ounces of bread* and drinking a comparable amount of water [each day and only] one *sextarius** of olive oil a year.

*5 *unciae* = 100–125 g.

*1/16th of a modius, ca. 567 cc.

3. Another spiritual discipline of his: he resolved to master sleep, and he recounted that he did not go under a roof for twenty days. He was burned by the noontide heat and bitten by the cold at night, in order to overcome sleep. He would say, "If I had not gone in under a roof so soon and gotten some sleep, my brain would have been so desiccated that eventually I would have been driven to distraction. I did conquer sleep insofar as it was up to me, but insofar as it depended on my nature (which has need of sleep) I gave in."

4. When he was sitting in his cell one morning a mosquito landed on his foot and stung him. This hurt him, so he squashed it with his hand, [releasing] a flood of blood. Recognizing that he had avenged himself, he sentenced himself to remain naked for six months by the marsh of Scete (which is in the great desert), where the mosquitoes pierce even the skins of wild boars, for they are like wasps. He was pierced all over, and this produced such swellings that some thought he had elephantiasis. When he came back to his cell six months later it was by his voice that it was known that he was Macarius.

5. As he told us himself, he once got the idea of going into the garden tomb of Jannès and Jambrês.* That garden tomb was from the magi who held power at that time under the Pharaoh. As they had acquired power for a long time, they built the work

*see Monks 21.5–12 for a different version of this story

with squared stones, making a monument to themselves there. They added much gold and planted trees, as the place is damp; they also dug a well.

6. Since the holy one did not know the way, he followed the stars with a certain amount of guesswork, traveling the desert as they do the high seas. He also took a sheaf of reeds and set one up indicating each mile so he could find the way when he came back. When he had been traveling for nine days he came near to the place, but the demon (who is always working against those who strive for Christ) gathered up all the reeds and put them beside his head while he was sleeping—about a mile from the garden tomb.

7. He found the reeds when he got up; maybe God had permitted this in order to further his training, in order that he might not put his trust in reeds but in the pillar of cloud that led Israel for forty years in the wilderness.* He used to say, "Seventy demons came out of the garden tomb to meet me, shouting and flying in my face like crows, saying, 'What do you want, Macarius? What do you want, monk? Why have you come to our place? You cannot stay here.' I said to them," he said, "I only want to come in and look around, then I am going away."

*Exod 33:9; Neh 9:19

8. "In I went," he said, "and found a small bronze pitcher hanging by an iron chain down the well; the rest was destroyed by time. The pomegranates had nothing inside them, having been dried out by the sun." So on the return journey he traveled twenty days; when the water he was carrying was exhausted, and the loaves, he was in great distress. He was at the point of collapse when—as he told

us—a maiden appeared to him dressed in clean linen, holding a dripping bottle of water

9. and standing (as he said) about a furlong away from him. For three days he traveled, seeing her with the bottle standing there but unable to catch up with her, as it is in dreams. Having endured patiently in the hope of drinking, he was empowered. After her a herd of buffalo appeared to him; a female with a young one came to a halt (there are many buffalo in those parts), and (as he said) her udder was flowing with milk. He got beneath her and was relieved by sucking her. The buffalo came as far as his cell, suckling him while not letting her calf near her.

10. Then again, another time, while he was digging a well near some dry twigs, he was bitten by an asp, a deadly animal. He took it up in his two hands, held it by the jaws and tore it apart, saying to it, "Since God did not send you, how did you dare to come?" He had various cells in the desert: one at Scete in the inner part of the great desert, one at Liba,* one at what is called The Cells, and one at the Mountain of Nitria. Some of them were without windows; he was said to spend Lent there in darkness. One was so small he could not stretch out his feet; another was larger; there he would meet those who were visiting him.

*location unknown

11. This man healed such a quantity of persons possessed of demons that it is not possible to state a number. While we were there, a noble spinster was brought from Thessalonica, who had been paralyzed for many years. Using his own hands, he anointed her with holy oil and prayed for over twenty days, then sent her back to her own city,

healed. When she got back she sent him offerings in great profusion.

12. When he heard that the folk at Tabennesi had a great way of life, he disguised himself, taking on the appearance of a working-class secular person. He traveled the desert for fifteen days and came to the Thebaid. When he got to the monastery* of the folk at Tabennesi, he sought out their archimandrite, whose name was Pachomius,* a man of great experience who had the spiritual gift of prophecy; it was hidden from him who and what Macarius was. When he encountered him, Macarius said to him, "I beg of you to take me into your monastery* so I may become a monk."

*askêtêrion

*ca. 292–346

*monê

13. Said Pachomius to him, "Anyway, you are advanced in age and cannot undertake spiritual discipline. The brothers practice it; you won't endure their toil. You'll be offended and go off speaking ill of them," and he did not take him in either the first or the second day. This went on for seven days, but Macarius persisted, fasting, and finally he said to Pachomius, "Take me in, abba, and if I do not fast and work as they do, order me to be thrown out." Then Pachomius persuaded the brothers to take him in among them. Now the population of the one monastery is fourteen hundred men to this day.

14. So in he went. A short time went by, and Lent was at hand; Macarius saw that each one practiced spiritual discipline by a different way of life; one ate in the evening, one every second evening, one every fifth. Then again, one stood all night long and then sat during the day. So Macarius steeped a large quantity of palm fronds and stood in a corner; he touched neither bread nor

water until the days of Lent had run their course and Easter had come and gone. He neither bent his knees nor reclined. He would take nothing but a few leaves of cabbage, and that on Sunday—to give the impression that he was eating.

15. If ever he went out for personal needs he quickly came in and took up his position, neither speaking to anybody nor opening his mouth but standing in silence. Apart from the prayer in his heart and the fronds in his hands he did nothing. When all the monks* had seen, they rose up against the higoumen, saying, "From where did you bring us this fleshless man to condemn us? Either get rid of him or be aware that we are all taking off." So when Pachomius heard the details of Macarius's way of life, he prayed to God for it to be revealed to him who this was.

*askêtai

16. It was revealed to him, and, taking Macarius's hand, he led him into the house of prayer where the altar was, saying to him, "Come now, venerable one: you are Macarius, and you concealed it from me; I have longed to see you for many years. I am grateful to you for smiting my children—so they do not have a high opinion of their spiritual discipline. Do you now go to your own place (for you have sufficiently edified us) and pray for us"—so Macarius went away as requested.

17. Another time he also related, "Having practiced correctly every way of life I wanted to, then another desire came upon me: I desired to keep my mind focused only on God without distraction for five or so days. Once I decided to do this I closed my cell and the courtyard so as not to answer to anybody. There I stood, beginning on the Monday,

instructing my mind: 'Do not come down from heaven; there you have angels and archangels, the higher powers and the God of all; do not come down lower than heaven.'

18. "I lasted two days and two nights and so aggravated the demon that he became a flame of fire and burned up everything in my cell. Even the mat on which I was standing was consumed by fire, and I thought I was being wholly incinerated. In the end I desisted on the third day without having succeeded in making my mind undistracted. I came down to contemplate the world so that it would not be reckoned a conceit in me."

19. I once visited the holy Macarius, and I found a village priest lying outside his cell. His head had been all devoured by the condition called cancer; the very bone of the skull could be seen. He was there to be healed, but Macarius would not grant him an interview. So I begged him, "Take pity on him, I beseech you, and give him an answer."

20. He said to me, "He is not worthy to be healed; a punishment has been given him. If you want him to be healed, persuade him to abstain from celebrating the liturgy; he is committing *porneia* and celebrating; that is why he is being punished. God is healing him." When I spoke to the sick man he agreed that he would no longer celebrate the liturgy—and swore to it. Then Macarius let him in and said to him, "Do you believe that there is a God?" "Yes," he said.

21. "And you were not able to deceive God?" "No," he answered. Macarius {said to him}, "If you acknowledge your sin and the punishment you received from God whereby you suffered this,

amend your behavior in the future." He confessed the fault and gave his word neither to sin anymore nor to celebrate the liturgy but to espouse the lay state. Then Macarius laid his hand on him, and he was healed within a few days. His hair grew back, and he went away whole.

22. Before my very eyes a small child was brought to Macarius, a child who was possessed of an evil spirit. Macarius placed one hand on its head and the other on the heart and prayed so long that he made it hang up in the air. The child swelled up like a wineskin and was so inflamed that it was entirely taken over by erysipelas. Then suddenly it cried out and discharged water from all its orifices. Having recovered, it resumed the size it was before. When Macarius had anointed it with holy oil and poured water over it, he gave it back to its father, directing him not to touch meat or wine for forty days. In this way he healed it.

23. Once Macarius was assailed by temptations of vainglory driving him out of his cell and suggesting that, since the end justifies the means, he go to the city of the Romans to heal the sick, for the spiritual gift against spirits was extremely effective in him. For a long time he paid no heed (although he was greatly moved); then, falling down at the threshold of his cell and leaving his feet outside, he said, "Drag and pull, demons, for I am not going away on my own feet. If you can bear me away like that, I will depart." He swore to them, "I am lying here until evening and, if you do not move me, I will not listen to you."

24. He got up after lying there a long time, and, when night drew on, they laid into him again. He

*about 16 liters

filled a basket with two *modii** of sand, placed it on his shoulders, and went walking through the desert. Theosebius the sweeper met him (an Antiochene by race) and said to him, "What are you carrying, abba? Allow me to take your burden and don't trouble yourself," but he said to him, "I am troubling the one who is troubling me; being out of control, he is whispering to me about going away." After he had walked a great deal he entered his cell, physically exhausted.

25. This holy Macarius told us (for he was a priest), "I noted at the time of distributing the mysteries that I never gave the offering to Mark the monk:* an angel used to give to him from the altar, but I only saw the wrist of the hand of the one who gave. This Mark was on the young side; he was memorizing the Old and New Testaments; he was exceedingly meek and more discreet than anybody else."

**askêtês*

26. One day toward the end of Macarius's long life, having some time to spare, I went and seated myself at his door, listening to what he was saying and doing, for I reckoned a man of his years to be an outstanding person. He was all alone in there, already almost a hundred years old, his teeth all gone, and he was fighting with the devil and himself, saying, "What do you want, wicked old thing? Here you have been into the oil and taken some wine; what else do you want, you old eater?"—he was upbraiding himself. Then to the devil, "Do I owe you anything now? You will not find anything; get away from me!" And as though prattling to himself, he said, "Come on, old eater, how long shall I be with you?"

27. Paphnoutius,* his disciple, told us, "One day a hyena took her youngster (which was blind) and brought it to Macarius. Pushing the gate of the courtyard, in she came. He was sitting outside, and she threw the youngster under his feet. Taking it up, the holy one spat on its eyes and prayed: suddenly it saw again. Its mother fed it, then picked it up and went away."

**Lausiac History* 47

28. Next day it brought the fleece of a large sheep to the holy one. As the blessed Melania said to me, "I received that fleece from Macarius as a mark of friendship," and why is it remarkable if he who calmed the lions for Daniel gave understanding to a hyena too? He used to say that from the time he was baptized he did not spit on the ground; it was then sixty years since he was baptized.

29. In appearance he was small of stature, beardless, with hair only on his lip and the point of the chin. Through his excessive spiritual discipline no hair grew on his cheeks. Once when I was afflicted with *accidie* I went to him and said to him, "What am I to do, abba, for temptations are afflicting me, saying, 'You are achieving nothing; get away from here.'" He said to me, "Tell them, 'I am keeping the walls for Christ.'" I have indicated to you these few of the many [things that are said] about the holy Macarius.

19. MOSES THE ETHIOPIAN

1. A person of the name of Moses was an Ethiopian by race, and he was black.[15] He was a slave

[15] Once a slave, Moses had been sent away by his master for thieving. He became a murderer and the chief of a robber

to some official, but his master got rid of him on account of his seriously evil disposition and brigandage; it was said that he had even committed murders. I have to speak of the details of his wickedness in order to demonstrate the virtue of his repentance. They say that he was the chief of one robber band; [this] deed of his is clearly among those of a brigand. He held a grudge against a shepherd who, with his dogs, had once frustrated him in some nocturnal adventure.

2. Moses wanted to kill the shepherd, so he investigated the place where he kept his sheep and was informed that it was at the other side of the Nile. Now the river was in flood, about one mile wide. Gripping his sword with his teeth, he put his little tunic on his head and crossed over like that, swimming the river. But while he was swimming across, the shepherd was able to escape notice by burying himself in the sand. Moses slaughtered four of the best rams, tied them with a rope, and swam back.

3. When he came to a small courtyard he skinned and ate the best of the rams and sold the fleeces for wine, of which he drank a measure (equal to eighteen Italian *sextarii*).* Then he went off to where he kept his band, fifty miles away. Somewhat later in life, the kind of a man he was notwithstanding, he became conscience stricken as a result of some eventuality. He surrendered himself to a monastery and thus proceeded to the business of repentance

*about 9 liters

band, but he had a change of heart, as a result of which he became an exemplary monk at Scete. He was slaughtered by the Mazics in 407–408, aged seventy-five, having refused to flee from their attack. See Cassian, Conf 1, 2. There are thirteen sayings attributed to Moses in APalph.

{so as to bring to an immediate knowledge of Christ the demon that had been his co-operator in evil from his youth up and his fellow sinner}. It is said that some brigands once fell on him when he was staying in his cell, unaware who he was; there were four of them.

4. He tied them all up, threw them on his back like a bag of chaff, and brought them to the brothers' church, saying, "Since it is not permitted for me to harm anybody, what do you want me to do with these?" As for them, they confessed their fault, and, when they realized that Moses was that one who was once so famous and renowned among brigands, they glorified God, and, inspired by his transformation, they too renounced the world, saying to themselves, "If this man who was once so influential and powerful among brigands feared God, why should we delay salvation?"

5. The demons attacked this Moses, drawing him toward his customary licentious practice of *porneia*. As he told it, he was so tempted that he was nearly wrecked in his determination. He came to Isidore the Great at Scete and poured out the matter of the battle. Isidore said to him, "Do not be dismayed; these are early days, so they attacked you the more fiercely, searching for your habitual behavior.

6. "A dog habitually in at a butcher's does not go far away, but if the butcher's is closed and nobody gives him anything, he does not hang around anymore. So it is with you; if you remain constant, the devil becomes bored and has to go away from you." Moses went his way and from that moment engaged in even more severe spiritual discipline,

especially concerning food. He ate nothing apart from dried bread, twelve ounces* a time, working very hard and offering fifty prayers [per day]. Although he afflicted his miserable body, he was still burning up and subject to dreams.

*twelve *unciae*, about 300 g.

7. Again, he visited one of the holy ones and said to him, "What am I to do, for the dreams of my soul are clouding my thinking in accordance with the pleasures I habitually enjoyed?" He said to him, "You are causing this because you have not separated your mind from visions of those [delights]. {Devote yourself to vigils and pray vigilantly; then you will quickly be rid of those}." Having heard this advice, he went into his cell and resolved not to sleep all night long or to bend his knee.

8. For six years he stayed in his cell, standing in prayer all the nights long in the middle of his cell, not closing an eye, but he did not succeed in overcoming the problem. So he proposed another way of life to himself. Setting out at night, he went off to the cells of the elders who were more advanced in spiritual discipline and, taking their water pots, discreetly filled them with water. They were some distance from the water, too: some of them two miles, some five, some just half a mile.

9. One night the demon who had been looking out for him but had run out of patience dealt him a blow on the loins with some sort of club as he was leaning over the well and left him for dead; he had no idea what had happened to him or at whose hands. Somebody came to draw water next day and found him lying there. He reported this to Isidore the Great, the priest of Scete—who took him up and brought him into the church. He was

so sick for a whole year that his body and soul hardly had any strength.

10. So Isidore the Great said to him, "Moses, stop contending with the demons and do not trample on them; there are limits to the courage [required in] spiritual discipline too," but he said, "I will not stop until the vision of demons ceases." Isidore said to him, "In the name of Jesus Christ, your dreams have ceased; make your communion with confidence. It was for your own good that you were held in subjection so that you would not boast of having mastered a passion,"

11. and he went off to his cell again. Afterward, maybe two months later, when Moses was asked by Isidore, he said he had not suffered anything more. He was deemed worthy of such a spiritual gift against demons that we fear those bluebottles more than he feared demons. That then is the way of life of Moses the Ethiopian, who was himself numbered among the great ones of the fathers. He became a priest and died at Scete aged seventy-five, leaving seventy disciples.

20. PAUL

1. There is a mountain called Phermê in Egypt, on the way to the great desert of Scete. About five hundred men are living on that mountain, practicing spiritual discipline. Among them is one named Paul, and this was his way of life. He did not set his hand to work or to trade, nor did he take anything from anybody other than the wherewithal to eat, for his task and his spiritual discipline were to pray without ceasing. He had three hundred stipulated

prayers; he collected that number of pebbles and had them in his bosom, then threw one pebble out of his bosom at each prayer.

*Macarius the Alexandrine

2. Visiting the holy Macarius (the one called the city dweller)* for an interview, he said to him, "Abba Macarius, I am afflicted." Macarius obliged him to say for what reason, and he told him, "There is a spinster living in a village who has practiced spiritual discipline for thirty years, and they tell me about her that she never eats except on Saturday and Sunday. Then, passing all the remaining five days of the week without eating, she offers seven hundred prayers. I despaired of myself {on learning this}, for I was unable to offer more than three hundred."

3. The holy Macarius replied to him, "For sixty years I have been offering one hundred stipulated prayers, while working for my food and having the necessary contact with the brothers—and my conscience is not accusing me of neglect. If you who offer three hundred are accused by your conscience, it is clear that you are not praying them purely, or are able to pray more and are not doing so."

21. EULOGIUS AND THE CRIPPLE

1. Cronius, the priest of Nitria, told me, "As a young man suffering an attack of *accidie* I fled the monastery of my archimandrite, wandered around, and came to the mountain[16] of the holy Antony, located between Babylon* and Heraclea,

*Fustat, near Cairo

[16] Mount Pispir, to the east of the Nile, about fifty miles south of Memphis, Antony's retreat.

in the great desert stretching along the Red Sea, about thirty miles from the river.* I came to his monastery located on the river at a place called Pispir, where his disciples Macarius and Amatas were living, the ones who buried him when he died, and there I waited around for five days to meet the holy Antony.

*the Nile

2. "He was said to visit this monastery for the benefit of those who happened to be there sometimes every ten days, sometimes every twenty days, sometimes every five days, depending on how God was guiding him. So different brothers congregated there, having a diversity of needs. Among them was a certain Eulogius, an Alexandrine who lived alone, and another who was a cripple; they too were there for the following reason.

3. "This Eulogius was an advocate with a general education. Prompted by a desire for immortality, he renounced the disturbances [of the world] and distributed all his possessions, leaving himself a few pieces of gold since he was incapable of working. Weary of his own company and neither willing to enter a community nor really confident of being alone, he found a cripple thrown down in the marketplace who had neither hands nor feet. Only his tongue was intact, to the misfortune of those who came by.

4. "Eulogius stood looking at him and praying to God. He made this covenant with God: 'Lord, I am going to take this cripple in your name, and I shall care for him until death so that I too may be saved through him. Grant me patient endurance in ministering to him.' Then he approached the cripple and said to him, 'O great one, do you want

me to take you home and to care for you?' 'Very much,' he said. 'Shall I then get an ass and take you?' said Eulogius, and so it was agreed. When he had brought an ass, taken him up, and carried him off to his own guest room, he began taking care of him.

5. "Nursed by Eulogius, the cripple lived on for fifteen years, washed and tended by his hands and fed as an invalid should be. But after fifteen years a demon got into him and caused him to revolt against Eulogius. He began dressing him down with such insulting and contemptuous expressions as, 'Cretin, runaway [slave], you have stolen funds not yours—and you want to be saved through me! Throw me into the market place: I want some meat.' He brought him meat.

6. "He cried out some more, 'I am not satisfied. I want the crowds; I want the marketplace. O what violence! Throw me where you found me,' and, if he had possessed hands, he might well have throttled Eulogius, the demon had so enraged him. At that Eulogius went to his neighbors who practiced spiritual discipline and said to them, 'What am I to do, for this cripple has brought me to despair? Shall I throw him out? I gave my promise to God, and I am afraid, but shall I not throw him out? He gives me bad days and nights; I just do not know what to do with him.'

7. "They said to him, 'The great one is still living'—for that was what they used to call Antony. 'Go to him; put the cripple in a boat and take him to the monastery. Wait there until Antony comes out of his cave and leave the decision to him. And whatever he says to you, be satisfied with his

verdict, for God is speaking to you through him.' Trusting them, he put the cripple in a small rustic boat, left the city by night, and brought him to the monastery of holy Antony's disciples."

8. Now (as Cronius related) it fell out that the great one came the next day, late in the evening, wrapped in a sheepskin mantle. When he came to their monastery it was his custom to summon Macarius and to question him: "Did some brothers come here, brother Macarius?" "Yes," he would reply. "Are they from Egypt or Jerusalem?"—for he had given a sign to them: "If you see that they are of small account, say 'from Egypt,' but say 'from Jerusalem' when they are more devout and erudite."

9. So he asked him in the usual way, "Are the brothers from Egypt or Jerusalem?" and in reply Macarius said to him, "They are a mixed bag." When he would say to him, "From Egypt," holy Antony used to say to him, "Prepare some lentils and give them that to eat." Then he would offer one prayer and send them on their way. But when he said, "They are from Jerusalem," he would sit there all night long talking to them about salvation.

10. According to Cronius, on that particular evening Antony sat down and summoned all the visitors. Nobody had said to him what the visitor's name was, and it was dark. Antony called out, saying, "Eulogius, Eulogius, Eulogius" three times, but that advocate did not reply, thinking some other Eulogius was being called. Antony spoke to him again: "Eulogius, I am talking to you, the one who has come from Alexandria." Said Eulogius to him, "I pray you, what is your command?" "Why have you come?" In reply, Eulogius said to him,

"He who revealed my name to you revealed my purpose too."

11. Antony said to him: "I know why you came, but speak out in the presence of all the brothers, so they too may hear." Eulogius told him, "I found this cripple in the marketplace and gave an undertaking to God that I would care for him, so that I might be saved through him and he through me. Since after so many years he has distressed me to the limit and I considered throwing him out—for this reason I came to your holiness so you could advise me what I ought to do and pray for me, for I am seriously distressed."

12. Antony spoke to him with a grave and severe voice, "Throw him out? But he who made him does not throw him out. You would throw him out? God will raise up one better than you and he will take him up." Eulogius was silent and reproved. Leaving Eulogius aside, Antony now began to give the cripple a tongue-lashing, shouting at him,

13. "Crippled, disabled, unworthy of earth and heaven, will you not stop resisting God? Are you not aware that it is Christ who is tending you? How dare you utter such things against Christ? Is it not on Christ's account that Eulogius enslaved himself in your service?" And having upbraided him, he turned away and spoke to all the rest of them according to their need. Then he turned back to Eulogius and the cripple and said to them,

14. "Travel around no more; go back and do not separate from each other, nowhere but in your cell in which you were for so long, for God is already sending for you. This trial came upon you when

you are both coming to the end, and you are going to be counted worthy of crowns. Do nothing else, lest when the angel comes he not find you in your place." Traveling in haste they came to their own cell; within forty days Eulogius died, and within another three days the cripple died.

15. When he had spent some time in the places around the Thebaid, Cronius went back to the monasteries of Alexandria, and it came about that the fortieth-day commemoration of the one and the third-day commemoration of the other were observed by the brotherhood. Cronius was amazed on learning this; he took a gospel and placed it in the midst of the brothers. Then with a solemn oath he declared what had happened: "I was the interpreter of all this conversation, as the blessed Antony does not know Greek. As I understood both languages I interpreted for them, in Greek to them, in Egyptian to him."

16. Cronius related this too: "During that night the blessed Antony told us this, too. 'A whole year long I prayed that the place of the righteous and of the sinners be revealed to me, and I saw a huge giant, high as the clouds and black. He had his hand stretched out to heaven, and beneath him there was a lake the size of a sea and I saw souls, flying like birds.

17. " 'Those flying above his hands and his head were being saved; they that were struck by his hands were falling into the lake. A voice came to me saying, "Those souls that you see flying above are the souls of the righteous, the ones that are being brought safely into Paradise; the others are they that are being dragged down to Hades,

having followed the desires of the flesh and the
Vita A 66.1–5 remembrance of injuries." ' "

22. PAUL THE SIMPLE[17]

1. Cronius related this too (so did the holy Hierax and many others of whom I am going to speak) about a rustic farmer named Paul, a simple man wholly without guile. He was married to a most beautiful wife who had a malicious disposition; she had been secretly indulging in sin for a very long time. Coming in from the field unexpectedly, Paul found them *in flagrante delicto*. Providence, however, was guiding him to do that which was to his advantage. Laughing gently, he called to them, saying, "All right, all right; it really doesn't matter to me. By Jesus, I am not taking her any more. Go on, you have her and her children; I am going off to be a monk."

2. Without saying a word to anybody he rapidly covered the eight stages [of the journey], came to the blessed Antony, and knocked at the door. Antony then came out and asked him, "What do you want?" "I want to become a monk," he said, and in reply Antony said to him, "You, a sixty-year-old man, cannot become a monk here. Rather, go into the village and work; live a worker's life, giving thanks to God, for you could not endure the afflictions of the desert." The old man answered him back saying, "If you teach me something, I'll do that."

[17] There is a long anecdote concerning Paul the Simple in APalph, PG 65:381C–385B, APsys 18.26.

3. Said Antony to him, "I told you, you are old and you cannot. If you do indeed want to be a monk, go off to a coenobion of many brothers, who will be able to put up with your weakness. I live alone here, eating every five days and that because of hunger." With these and such like words he tried to scare Paul away, but as he was not accepting his advice, Antony shut the door and did not come out on his account (not even because of need) for three days. But Paul did not go away.

4. Compelled by need, Antony opened on the fourth day. He came out again and said to him, "Get away from here, old man; why are you troubling me? You cannot stay here." Paul said to him, "It is impossible for me to die anywhere but here." Antony looked him over and, noticing that he was not carrying anything to eat, neither bread nor water, realized that he had lasted to the fourth day fasting. "Perhaps he will die and defile my soul," he said, and he took him in. Now in those days Antony had embraced a way of life such as he would never have had when he was young.

5. He dampened some fronds and said to Paul, "Here, braid some rope as I do." The old man braided away until the ninth hour, toiling to produce fifteen fathoms.* Antony was not pleased when he saw this; he said to him, "You have braided badly; unbraid it and braid it all over again." He inflicted this unpleasant task on him who was fasting and advanced in years so that the old man would get angry and run away from Antony. But he unbraided and braided the same fronds, even though it was more difficult, as they had become wrinkled.* When Antony saw that he neither complained nor became

*about 30 m.

*i.e., dried out

faint hearted nor was irritated, he was pricked in his conscience.

6. When the sun had gone down, Antony said to him, "Do you want us to eat a bit of bread?" "As you wish, abba," Paul said to him, and this too swayed Antony: that he did not come running eagerly at the announcement of food but referred the decision to him. So he set up the table and brought out some bread. Antony put down the loaves, each about six ounces,* and dampened one of them for himself (for they were dry) but three for Paul. Then Antony chanted a psalm he knew; he chanted it twelve times and prayed twelve times, in order to put Paul to the test.

*six *unciae*, about 160 g.

7. But Paul eagerly prayed along with him, for, in my opinion, he would have preferred being a shepherd of scorpions to living with an adulterous woman. After the twelve prayers they sat down to eat when the evening was far advanced; Antony ate one of the loaves but did not touch another. The old man was eating in a more leisurely fashion and still had some of his loaf. Waiting until he had finished it, Antony said to him, "Eat another loaf, little father." Paul said to him, "If you eat, so will I, but not if you are not eating." Antony said to him, "That is enough for me, for I am a monk."

8. Said Paul to him, "It is enough for me too, for I too want to become a monk." Antony got up again and offered twelve prayers and chanted twelve psalms. He slept a little, the first sleep, then rose again to chant psalms from midnight to daybreak. Seeing the old man eagerly following him step by step in his way of life, he said to him, "If you can be like that day by day, stay with

me." Paul said to him, "If there is anything more I don't know, since I will easily do those things I saw." Next day Antony said to him, "See, you have become a monk."

9. After a certain number of months Antony became convinced that Paul was spiritually mature and quite uncomplicated. Since the grace of God was working with him, he built him a cell three or four miles away and said to him, "Here; now you have become a monk, stay by yourself so you can experience the onslaught of demons." When he had lived there one year, Paul was deemed worthy of the spiritual gift against demons and illnesses. For example, one day there was brought to Antony an excessively terrifying person with a ruling spirit of demonic powers, who would even blaspheme against heaven itself.

10. Antony carefully examined him; then he said to those who brought him, "This is not a task for me; I have not yet been deemed worthy of a spiritual gift against this class of ruling [demons]—this is for Paul." So off went Antony and took them to Paul. He said to him, "Abba Paul, throw this demon out of the man so he can go back to his own [folk] healed." Paul said to him, "What about you?" and Antony said to him: "I do not have time; I have other work"—he left him and went back to his own cell.

11. So the old man stood up, offered a fervent prayer, and then addressed the demon: "Abba Antony has said to you, 'Get out of the man.'" The demon, however, cried out blasphemously, "I am not coming out, wicked old man," but Paul took his sheepskin and struck him on the back,

saying, "Abba Antony has said, 'Get out.' " Now the demon insulted both Antony and him again, more vigorously. Finally Paul said to the demon, "Out you go, or I am going to tell Christ. By Jesus, if you do not get out right away I am going to tell Christ, and he will make it the worse for you."

12. The demon renewed his blasphemous language, crying out, "I am not coming out." Enraged against the demon, Paul went out of the guesthouse at midday when the sun was at zenith; the heat among the Egyptians is like the furnace of Babylon. Standing on a rock in the mountain he prayed, speaking like this: "Jesus Christ, you who were crucified under Pontius Pilate, behold: I am not coming down from this rock; I am not eating or drinking until I die if you do not cast the spirit out of the man and set the man free."

13. Before all the words had got out of his mouth, the demon shouted out, "Oh, what violence! I am being driven out! The simplicity of Paul is driving me: where am I to go?" And straightaway the spirit came out and was transformed into a great dragon seventy cubits long dragging itself into the Red Sea, so that what was said might be fulfilled: "The righteous shall proclaim a faith that
Prov 12:17 reveals itself." This is the wonder of Paul who was called "the simple" by all the brotherhood.

23. PACHÔN

1. There was a man living at Scete who had reached seventy years of age; his name was Pachôn. Now it happened that I was being troubled by the desire for a woman, and I was distressed in the

matter both by my thoughts and by nocturnal visions. I was close to abandoning the desert (as the passion was leading me on), and I did not reveal the matter to my neighbors or to Evagrius, my teacher. I secretly took to the great desert, and for a fortnight I was meeting with the aged fathers of Scete in the desert.

2. Among them I encountered Pachôn, too. Realizing that he was even purer and more disciplined, I got up the courage to reveal to him what was on my mind. He said to me, "Do not let the matter surprise you; you are not suffering this from idleness. The place, the scarcity of the necessities of life there, and the absence of contact with women attest in your favor. Your problem is rather due to your zeal. The battle with *porneia* has three aspects: sometimes the flesh, being robust, afflicts us, sometimes the passions through our thoughts, sometimes the demon himself does it by malign influence. This I have discovered myself from much close observation.

3. "Look, as you can see, I am an old man; I have spent forty years in this cell, taking thought for my own salvation, and, reaching this age, I have been tempted to this point." And he attested, "For twelve years after my fiftieth year there was no letup in the assault on me by night or by day. I suspected that God had abandoned me and I was being overcome for that reason. I preferred to die without reason rather than to be deformed by a carnal passion. Off I went and, going around in the desert, found a hyena's cave. I positioned myself, naked, before that cave by day so the beasts would eat me when they came out.

4. "When evening drew on, as it is written, 'You make darkness and it becomes night; all the beasts
Ps 103:20 of the forest move about in it,' out came the beasts, the male and the female. They smelled me from head to feet, licking me; I was fully expecting to be eaten—and then they went away from me. I lay there all night and was not eaten. Reckoning that God had spared me, I went back to my cell again. After delaying a few days the demon attacked me again, more forcefully than at first, until I was at the point of blaspheming.

5. "He transformed himself into an Ethiopian maiden whom I had once seen in my youth, gathering reeds in summer. She sat on my knees and so excited me that I was thinking of making love with her. In my fury I struck her a blow, at which she became invisible: for two years I could not stand the stench of my hand. Discouraged and despairing, I went wandering in the great desert. Finding a small asp, I took it up and put to my genitals so that in that way I would be bitten and would die. I pressed the animal's head against my genitals (the cause of my temptation), but I was not bitten.

6. "Then I heard a voice that came into my thinking: 'Go back, Pachôn, fight on! It was for this reason that I left you to be dominated: so that you would not be proud of your strength but, recognizing your weakness and lacking the courage for your way of life, you would go running for the help of God.' Reassured by this, I turned back and confidently stayed; the battle was stilled for the rest of my life, for, aware of my disposition, it no longer came near me."

24. STEPHEN OF LIBYA

1. One Stephen, a Libyan by race, resided for sixty years on the shores of the Marmara and of Lake Mareotis. Reaching the pinnacle as one of spiritual discipline, he was deemed worthy of the spiritual gift of discretion, so that every aggrieved person who approached him, with no matter what grief, went away relieved of grief. He was also known to the blessed Antony, and he lived on into our own times, but I did not meet him myself on account of the remote location of his dwelling.

2. Persons of the entourage of the holy Ammônius and of Evagrius who had met him, however, told me, "We discovered that he had been afflicted by an illness in the very regions of his testicles and penis, and this illness had brought about an ulcer that is called a cancer. We found him being operated on by some doctor, but Stephen kept working with his hands, braiding palm fronds, and talking to us while the rest of his body was being handled. His disposition was such that it was as if someone else was being incised. His members were cut off like hairs, but he was insensitive because of an excess of godly preparation.

3. "As we grieved over this and felt disgust that such a life had fallen prey to a disease like that and to such interventions, he said to us, 'Do not be upset by this business, my sons; nothing God does is done with evil intent, but toward a beneficial end. And perhaps my members were liable to suffer punishment, and it is advantageous that they should pay the penalty right here rather than after leaving the arena.' Comforting and sustaining us in that way, he strengthened us." This

I have recounted so that when we see some holy persons falling into sufferings like that, we may not be perturbed.

25. VALENS

1. There was a person called Valens, a Palestinian by race but a Corinthian in character, for Saint Paul attributed the disease of self-importance to the Corinthians.* He reached the desert and lived with us for some years. He went so far in pride that he was beguiled by demons. By beguiling him a little at a time they made him have big ideas, such as that angels were in contact with him.

*1 Cor 4:18; 2 Cor 12:20

2. Then one day (as they recounted it), while he was working in the dark, he dropped the needle with which he was stitching a basket. As he could not find it, the devil made a lamp and found the needle. Thinking even more highly of himself at this, Valens had big ideas again; he became so self-important that he even spurned the mysteries of Holy Communion. Now it happened that some strangers had come, bringing some dried fruits into church for the brotherhood.

3. Our priest, the holy Macarius, took some and then sent up to a handful to each one of us in his cell, including Valens. Valens seized the one who brought them, upbraided him, and struck him, saying to him, "Go and tell Macarius, 'I am not your inferior for you to send me alms.'" Macarius realized that he was deluded; a day later he went to soothe him. He said to him "Valens, you were deluded; stop it." But as Valens would not listen to his exhortations, he went away.

4. Confident now that Valens was absolutely convinced by his deceit, off went the demon and disguised himself as the Savior, and he appeared by night in a vision of thousands of angels holding lamps and a wheel of fire, in which he appeared to represent the Savior. One preceded the others, saying, "Christ was enamored of your way of life and your confident way of living it. He has come to see you, so come out of your cell and do nothing more than fall down and worship him when you see him from afar, then go into your cell."

5. So out he went, and, on seeing the formation of lampholders and the Antichrist about a stade* away, he fell down and worshiped. Again the next day he was so raving mad that he went into the church and, when the brotherhood was assembled, said, "I do not need Communion, for I have seen Christ today." Then the fathers bound him and, putting him in irons, treated him over the course of one year and removed his self-conceit with prayers, indifferent food, and a less active life, as it is said, "Opposite cures for opposite."

*about 200 m.

6. Just as among the sacred plants of Paradise there was the tree of the knowledge of good and evil, I have to include the lives of people like that in this little book for the security against stumbling of those who read it, so that if ever some success befalls them, they do not become high-minded on account of that virtue. For virtue often becomes the occasion of a fall whenever it is not achieved with the right intention, as it is written, "I have seen the righteous man perish in his righteousness, and this too is vanity."*

*Eccl 7:15

26. HÊRON

*see *Lausiac History* 47.4; Cassian, Conf 2.5

1. A person named Hêron* became my neighbor, an Alexandrine by race, a young bourgeois with a sharp mind and a pure life, but he too, after many labors, was afflicted with conceit and thrown headlong. He looked down on the fathers, especially reviling the blessed Evagrius, saying, "They who are persuaded by your teaching are being led astray; we ought not to heed any teachers other than Christ." He employed the testimony [of Scripture] also to support the drift of his folly, saying, "The Savior himself said, 'Do not call anyone on earth teacher.' "[18]

2. He himself became so darkened that he was put in irons later on for not even wanting to approach the mysteries. But the truth must be told: his way of life was extremely austere, and, according to many who were acquainted with him, he often ate only every three months, being satisfied with the communion of the mysteries and wild cabbage, if some appeared anywhere. I too had experience of him on my way to Scete together with the blessed Alban.*

*see *Lausiac History* 47.3

3. Scete was forty miles away from us; in the course of those forty miles we ate bread twice and drank water three times, while Hêron took nothing. As he walked along he recited fifteen psalms, then the long one,* then the Epistle to the Hebrews, then Isaiah and part of Jeremiah, then the gospel of Luke, and then Proverbs. While that was happening, we could not keep up with him as he strode along.

*Ps 118

[18] "Do you [pl.] not be called *rabbi*, for one is your teacher [*didaskalos*]; you are all brothers."*

*Matt 23:8

4. In the end, as though driven by fire, he could no longer remain in his cell. Off he went to Alexandria by providence, and "he drove out the nail by a nail," as they say, for he willingly fell into moral indifference and later on found salvation unwillingly. For he began frequenting the theater and horse races and hanging around in taverns. Overeating and knocking back wine like this, he fell into the mire of wanting a woman.

5. While he was thinking about sinning, he encountered a prostitute and discussed his festering sore. This is how things were progressing when there appeared a carbuncle right on his penis, and he was so ill for a space of six months that his testicles rotted away and dropped off. He subsequently got better again (without those parts) and returned to a godly frame of mind. He came and confessed all this to the fathers, but he died within a few days without having resumed his way of life.

27. PTOLEMY

1. Yet another one, Ptolemy by name, lived a life that is difficult if not impossible to relate. He lived beyond Scete at what is called Klimax.* The place is so called because nobody can live there, the brothers' well being eighteen miles away. He carried many an amphora from there, and in December and January he used to collect the dew off the rocks with a sponge, for there is heavy dew in those parts at that time. He succeeded in living there for fifteen years.

*"ladder"; location unknown

2. But estranged from teaching, from the company, from the beneficial discourse of holy men,

and from frequent partaking of the mysteries, he diverged so far from the straight way as to say that those things were of no account. He became so unsettled that he went off wandering in Egypt to this day, delivering himself to overeating and knocking back wine, with not a word to anybody. And this misfortune befell Ptolemy from unreasonable conceit, as it is written: "Those who have no government fall like leaves."*

*Prov 2:14

28. THE FALLING SPINSTER

I also knew a spinster in Jerusalem who wore sackcloth for six years and lived enclosed, taking nothing of what might contribute to her pleasure, but subsequently she was abandoned for excessive pride and met with a fall. Opening her window, she admitted the man who looked after her and made love with him. For she was not keeping to her spiritual discipline following a godly purpose and love for God, but as a human display, composed of vainglory and an impure intention. As her thoughts were occupied in passing judgment on others, the guardian of continence was not in her.

29. ELIJAH

1. Elijah, whose spiritual discipline was severe, became quite devoted to spinsters—for there are such souls to whom the virtuous goal they pursue bears witness. Feeling compassion for the order of women who were practicing spiritual discipline, he built a large monastery in the city of Athrib,

where he owned some property. He gathered all the wandering women into the monastery, then went on caring for them. He secured their complete comfort, providing gardens, household utensils, and furniture, and whatever life requires. But, drawn as those women were from various ways of life, they were continually squabbling with each other.

2. Since he had to hear them out and pacify them (for he had gathered up about three hundred of them), he had to intervene for two years. Being a young man (he was thirty or forty years old), he was tempted to enjoy himself. He withdrew from the monastery and went wandering in the desert for two days, fasting, making this supplication: "Lord, either kill me so I do not see those afflicted women, or take the passion away from me so I can look after them rationally."

3. He fell asleep in the desert when evening fell, and three angels came to him (as he himself told it). Laying hold on him they said, "Why did you come out of the women's monastery?" He related the matter to them: "I was afraid of harming both them and myself." They said to him, "If we relieve you of the passion, will you go back and look after them?" He agreed to those terms, and they made him swear an oath.

4. The oath (he used to say) was like this, "Swear to us that by him who looks after me I will look after them," and he swore to them. Then they took hold of him, one his hands and one his feet; the third took a razor and cut off his testicles, not in reality, but in appearance. He seemed to be in an ecstasy, as you might say, and to have been cured. "Did you feel any benefit?" they asked him, and he told them, "I

was greatly relieved, and I do believe I am delivered from the passion."

5. They said to him, "Off you go." Returning after five days, he found the monastery in mourning. In he went, and there he stayed from then on in a cell to one side, from which (being close by) he was continually rectifying the women's behavior, insofar as he was able. He lived another forty years, and he firmly asserted to the fathers, "No passion arose in my mind." Such was the spiritual gift of that holy one who took such care of the monastery.

30. DOROTHEUS

His successor was Dorotheus, a man of great experience, who grew old living a life of goodness and activity. Unable to live in the monastery itself as Elijah had done, he shut himself up in an upper story and made a window (which he used to open and close) looking onto the women's monastery. He sat at that window all the time, guaranteeing them freedom from quarreling. He grew old doing this, up there on the upper story, with neither the women going up to him nor him being able to go down, for there was no ladder.

31. PIAMOUN

1. Piamoun was a spinster who lived with her own mother all the years of her life, eating every second day in the evening and spinning linen. She was deemed worthy of the spiritual gift of fore-

knowledge. For example, at one time, when the river in Egypt was in flood, village rose up against village. They were fighting so intensely about the sharing of water that death and devastation ensued. A more powerful village attacked the spinster's village; men came in numbers with spears and clubs to devastate her village.

2. But an angel appeared to her, revealing their onslaught to her. She summoned the village elders and said to them, "Go out and meet those who are coming against you from such-and-such a village, so that you may not be destroyed together with the village, and beg them to abandon their enmity." The elders were afraid; they fell at her feet, begging and saying to her, "We dare not confront them, for we know their drunkenness and madness.

3. "But if you will take pity on the whole village and on your house, go out yourself and meet them." She did not agree to that, but she went up onto her own roof by night and stood there praying all the time (not kneeling down) and beseeching God, "Lord, you who judge the earth and to whom nothing unjust is pleasing, when this prayer comes before you, may your power immobilize them at whatever place it finds them."

4. At about the first hour they were immobilized at a place about three miles away and were unable to stir. It was also revealed to them that it was through her intercessions that their impediment had come about. They sent to the village and sued for peace, exclaiming, "So give thanks to God and to the prayers of Piamoun—for they impeded us."

32. PACHOMIUS AND THOSE AT TABENNESI

1. There is a place called Tabennesi in the Thebaid, and that is where Pachomius lived, a man among those who lived righteously and so were deemed worthy of foreknowledge and of visions of angels. This man became immensely devoted to folk and to his brothers. While he was residing in the cave, an angel appeared to him and said, "You have set your own matters to rights; you live too much in the cave. Come on out; gather together all the young monks and live with them; lay down laws for them according to the rule that I am giving you." And he gave him a bronze tablet on which these things had been written:

2. "You shall allow each one to eat and to drink according to his energy. Entrust tasks to them in proportion to the energies of those who eat, and do not prevent them from either fasting or eating. Thus entrust the more vigorous tasks to those who are eating, the less demanding ones to the more spiritually disciplined. Build discreet cells in the courtyard and let them live three to a cell, but let them all look for their food in the one house.

3. "They are not to sleep lying down; let them sleep sitting up, having made chairs built with sloping backs, and put their covers on them. At night let them wear linen albs with a girdle. Let each have a cloak made from a goatskin, and let them not eat without it. When they go for Communion on Saturdays and Sundays, let them loosen the girdles and set aside the cloak; let them go in wearing only a cowl." He stipulated cowls for them without fleece, as for children, and ordered

the sign of the cross to be imprinted upon them in purple.

4. He ordered there to be twenty-four orders, and to each order he applied a letter of the Greek alphabet, alpha, beta, gamma, delta, etc. When he inquired about or did business with such a multitude, the superior asked his second in command, "How is the *alpha*-order?" or "How is it with the *zeta*?" or "My compliments to the *rho*." "Following some particular letter-sign you shall apply the letter *iota* to the more simple and guileless ones and apply the *xi* on the more complicated and difficult."

5. And in this way he accommodated the letter to each order according to the state of their intentions, their characters, and their lives, with only the spiritual knowing the significance. It had been written on the tablet, "A guest from another monastery that has another rule should neither eat nor drink with these; neither should he enter the monastery unless he is in the course of a journey. Him, however, who has entered to stay with them they do not admit into the inner chambers for three years. But when he has done some serious work, then he comes in after three years.

6. "Let them cover their heads with their cowls when they are eating so no one brother can see another chewing. They are not to speak while eating or to let their eyes wander anywhere beyond their plate or the table." [The tablet] stipulated that they were to offer twelve prayers in the course of the whole day, twelve in the evening, twelve during the vigils, and three at the ninth hour. And it stipulated that when the community was about to eat, a psalm was to be sung before each prayer.

7. When Pachomius protested to the angel that the prayers were few, the angel said to him, "I set the rule like that so that even the young ones can fulfill it and not grieve; the fully instructed ones have no need of direction. On their own in their cells they devoted their entire life to the contemplation of God. I laid down laws for those who do not have an understanding mind so that, fulfilling the ordering of the way of life, they might have a confident disposition."

8. There are several monasteries adhering to this rule, embracing seven thousand men. The first and great monastery, the one that brought the other monasteries into being, is where Pachomius himself lived; in it are 1300 men. Among them is the good Aphthonius, who has become my true friend and is now second in command at that monastery. There being no hint of scandal about him, they send him to Alexandria to sell their products and to purchase what they need.

9. There are other monasteries of two or three hundred, of which I entered the one in the city of Panos* and found three hundred men. {In that monastery I saw fifteen tailors, seven metalworkers, four carpenters, twelve camel drivers, and fifteen fullers. They practice every trade, supplying women's monasteries and prisons from their surplus products.

*Akhmîn today, on the right bank of the Nile in Upper Egypt

10. They raise hogs too; when I criticized this, they said, "We gathered from tradition that they should be raised on chaff, the remains of vegetables, and surplus goods that are thrown away, so these do not go to waste. The hogs should be slaughtered, the meat sold (the better cuts being

consumed by the sick and the aged), for the region is of moderate size and is well populated"—in fact the Blemmy tribe* lives close beside them.}

*Ethiopian nomads of the upper Nile

11. Those who are on duty for the day rise at dawn; some are in the kitchen, others in the refectory. They are at their posts, getting things ready until the appointed hour. They put loaves on the table, with mixed charlock, olives, vegetables, cheese from cows' milk, {the best cuts of meat,} and small vegetables. There are some who come to eat at the sixth hour, others at the seventh, others at the eighth, others at the ninth, and others at the eleventh, others late in the evening, others every second day. So each letter knows its appointed time.

12. So too were their tasks: one worked the earth as a farmer, another in the garden, another in the smithy, another in the bakery, and another in the carpenters' shop or the fullers' shop; another braided large baskets, another worked in the tannery or in the cobblers' shop or in the scriptorium, and another at braiding small baskets. But they were learning all the Scriptures by heart.

33. THE WOMEN'S MONASTERY

1. They also have a monastery for about four hundred women; these have the same rule and the same way of life except for the cloak. The women are across the river, the men at this side. When a sister dies, the sisters who have prepared her for burial bring her and lay her on the riverbank. The brothers cross over with a boat and take her to the other shore with palm and olive branches and psalm singing; then they bury her in their own tombs.

2. With the exception of the priest and the deacon (and they only on Sundays), nobody crosses to the women's monastery. An event like this took place in this women's monastery: a secular person who was a tailor in search of work crossed over in ignorance. A younger sister came out (for the place is desert) and unintentionally ran into him. "We have our own tailors," she told him.

3. Another sister witnessed this encounter. Time went by; then an altercation arose, and, by devilish supposition, from much perversity and seething rage, [the other sister] made a false accusation against the sister before the community, and a few other sisters gave their support to the accusation out of spite. Overcome with grief at being falsely accused of something that had never even entered her mind, that sister, unable to bear it, threw herself into the river when nobody was looking and perished.

4. She who had made the false accusation was aware that it was out of perversity that she had made the accusation and brought about this bloodletting. She went and hanged herself, unable to bear the matter. The remaining sisters declared the matter to the priest when he came, and he ordered that no offering of the Eucharist be made even for one of those two sisters. And as for those who had failed to reconcile them, since they were aware of the false accusation and had still given credence to what was said, he excommunicated them, imposing a period of seven years.

34. THE WOMAN WHO PRETENDED TO BE INSANE*

*see APsys 18.24, and Daniel of Scete 07, Bibliotheca 2101

1. In this monastery there was another sister who pretended to be insane and [possessed by] a demon. They loathed her so much that they would not even eat with her, and that was what she wanted. Wandering around the kitchen, she used to do all sorts of work, and she was the sponge of the monastery, as they say, fulfilling by her behavior that which is written: "If anyone among you seems to be wise in this world, let him become a fool in order to be wise."* She had bound a rag round her head (all the others were shorn and wore hoods), and that was how she served.

*1 Cor 3:18

2. Not one of the four hundred ever saw her eating during the years of her life; she did not sit at table, nor did she receive a piece of bread. She just sponged up the crumbs from the tables and washed the pots; that sufficed for her. She never insulted anybody, did not complain, did not speak a little or at length although she was punched and insulted, cursed and loathed.

3. An angel came to the holy Piteroum, a tried and tested anchorite living at Porphyrites,* and said to him, "Why do you have such a high opinion of yourself for being pious and living in such a place? Do you want to see a woman who is more devout than you? Go to the monastery of women at Tabennesi, and there you shall find one wearing a diadem on her head; she is better than you,

*between the Nile and the Red Sea

4. "for in competition with such a multitude she has never separated her heart from God—while you live here, wandering over cities in your mind." And he who never went out went to that monastery

and requested permission of the teachers to enter the women's monastery. Given his renown and his great age, they brought him with confidence.

5. When he came in, he requested to see them all; she did not appear. Finally he said to them, "Bring them all to me, for there is another missing." They said to him, "We have one who is a fool in the kitchen" (that is how they call the suffering ones). He said to them, "Bring her to me too; let me see her." They went to call her, but she would not obey; perhaps she discerned the situation or even had it revealed to her. They dragged her by force, saying to her, "Holy Piteroum wants to see you," for he was renowned.

6. When she came, he saw the rag on her brow, and falling at her feet, he said to her, "Bless me." She likewise fell at his feet and said to him, "Bless me, sir." They were all astounded and said to him, "Do not be offended, Abba—she is a fool." Piteroum said to them all, "It is you who are fools; this one is our *amma*" (that is what they call spiritual women), "and I pray to be found worthy of her on Judgment Day."

7. On hearing this, they fell at his feet, all confessing different things: one that she had poured the washbowl on her, another that she had punched her, another that she had rubbed her nose in mustard. In a word, they all confessed various offenses. When he had prayed for them he went his way. After a few days, unable to tolerate the esteem and respect of the sisters and weighed down by their excuses, she went out of the monastery. Where she went, where she hid away, or how she died, nobody knew.

35. JOHN OF LYCOPOLIS[19] [ASYUT]

1. There was one in Lycopolis named John who had learned carpentry in his youth; his brother was a dyer. Later on, when he reached the age of about twenty-five, he renounced [the world], and after he had passed five years in various monasteries, he withdrew alone to Mount Lycos. At its very summit he built himself three domed chambers, entered them, and walled himself in. One chamber was for the needs of the flesh, one where he worked and ate, the other where he prayed.

2. When he had been shut up there for thirty years, receiving the necessities of life through a window from somebody who looked after him, he was deemed worthy of the spiritual gift of foreknowledge. For instance, he sent several predictions to the blessed emperor Theodosius* concerning the usurper Maximus (that he would return from Gaul triumphant against him), and he proclaimed the good news concerning the usurper Eugenius.* John was widely acclaimed as a man of virtue.

*Theodosius I

*Theodosius suppressed Maximus in 388, Eugenius in 394

3. While we were in the Nitrian desert, I and those associated with the blessed Evagrius sought to learn precisely of what the virtue of the man consisted. The blessed Evagrius said, "It would please me to learn what kind of man this is from the one who knows how to evaluate mind and word. If I am unable to see him myself but can hear an accurate report of his way of life with another telling it, then I am not going off to the mountain."

[19] The first section of Monks deals with John at some length. He was probably born ca. 305 and spent forty years in seclusion (forty-eight, says Palladius, *Lausiac History* 35.13). Lycopolis is now Asyut or Assiout on the upper Nile, west bank.

I said nothing to anybody when I heard this but kept quiet for a day, but the next day I closed up my cell, entrusted myself to God, and gave myself the trouble of journeying as far as the Thebaid.

4. I arrived in eighteen days, having walked some of the way and then sailed on the river. It was the time the river floods, when many fall sick—as did I. So I came there and found his courtyard closed. The brothers later built a huge courtyard in which about a hundred men can be accommodated. They kept it locked with a key but would open it up on Saturday and Sunday. When I learned the reason that it had been closed, I possessed my soul in patience* until Saturday. Then I presented myself at the second hour for a meeting and found him sitting at the window, through which he seemed to confer encouragement on those who were visiting.

*Luke 21:19

5. He greeted me, then said through an interpreter, "Where are you from and why have you come? I am of the opinion that you are of Evagrius's company." "I am a foreigner from Galatia," I said, and confirmed that I was a companion of Evagrius. Meanwhile, as we were talking, the governor of the region came up, Alypius* by name. Hurrying to him, John broke off our conversation. I withdrew a little and gave them some room, standing at a distance. They spoke with each other at length, and I became bored, and, being bored, I complained about the monk for having contempt for me but respect for the governor.

*the vicar of Africa

6. Disgusted in my mind at this, I was thinking of going away in contempt of him, but he summoned the interpreter (Theodore by name) and

said to him, "Go and say to that brother, 'Do not be downhearted; I will dismiss the governor presently and speak with you.'" So, having regard for him as a spiritual man, I decided to continue waiting. When the governor came out, John called me and said to me, "Why did you take offense at me? What did you find offensive that you thought those things that are uncharacteristic of me and were inappropriate for you? Or are you not aware that it is written, 'It is not they who are healthy who have need of a physician, but those who are unwell?'* I can find you when I want to, and you me.

*Luke 5:31

7. "And if I do not comfort you, other brothers and other fathers will comfort you, whereas this man has been delivered to the devil on account of his worldly concerns. Gaining respite for a short time like a slave escaping from his master, he came to receive some benefit. It would have been improper to have abandoned him to spend time with you, you who are paying attention unceasingly to your salvation." I begged him to pray for me, convinced that he was a spiritual man.

8. Then with a smile he gave me a gentle blow on the left cheek with his right hand and said to me, "Many afflictions await you, and you were strongly tempted to leave the desert. You were terrified and you put it off, but the demon rekindles it, bringing religious arguments and fine words against you. He suggested a desire to see your father again and the instruction of your brother and sister in the monastic life.

9. "Look, I bring you good news. Both of them were saved, for they renounced [the world], and your father is going to live for some more years. So

persevere in the desert, and do not be wanting to go off to your homeland on their account, for it is written, 'No one who sets his hand to the plough and turns back is well adapted to the kingdom of heaven.'"* Having benefited from these words and been well reinvigorated, I gave thanks to God on learning that the factors leading me astray were eliminated.

*Luke 9:62

10. Then, jesting, he also said to me, "Do you want to be a bishop?"* "I am one," I said to him, and he said to me, "Where?" I said, "In kitchens, taverns, refectories, bottle-stores; I oversee* these, and if the wine is turned bitter, I set it aside but drink the good. In the same way I also oversee* the cooking pot, and if it is short of salt or any seasoning, I throw some in and season it—and eat it like that. That is my bishopric;* gluttony ordained me."

**episkopos*

**episkopô*

**episkopô*

**episkopê*

11. With a smile he said to me, "No more joking; you are going to be ordained bishop and to have much toil and affliction. If you would flee from afflictions, do not leave the desert, for nobody is going to ordain you bishop in the desert." Leaving him, I came to my usual place by way of the desert after reporting those very things to the blessed fathers, who, two months later, sailed off to meet him. But I forgot his words, for three years later I fell sick with a sickness of the spleen and of the stomach.

12. I was sent by the brothers from there to Alexandria after showing symptoms of dropsy. The physicians advised me to leave Alexandria for Palestine to take the air, for the air is light there and suitable for my condition. From Palestine I went to Bithynia, and there, I know not how, whether from human effort or the good will of the one who is

superior (God would know), I was deemed worthy of ordination—after becoming involved in the situation concerning the blessed John [Chrysostom].

13. Shut away for eleven months in a gloomy cell, I recalled that those things of which that blessed [John of Lycopolis] forewarned me were now happening. And this he told me, intending to bring me to patient endurance in the desert by the narrative, "I have been forty-eight years in this cell. I have not seen the face of a woman nor had the sight of a piece of gold. I did not see anybody chewing, and nobody saw me eating or drinking."

14. This man did not meet with the servant of God Poimenia when she came to see him, but he did reveal some mystical secrets to her. He instructed her not to go by way of Alexandria when she was returning to the Thebaid, "for you will fall into temptation," but she either disagreed or forgot and turned toward Alexandria to see the city. As they journeyed, her flotilla tied up near Nicopolis* for some repose.

*halfway between Memphis and Alexandria

15. The servants disembarked and, as a result of some disorderliness, got into a fight with the local folk, who were crazy people. They took a finger off one who was a eunuch, killed another, and immersed the most holy Bishop Dionysius (whom they did not recognize) in the river. As for her, they crushed her with abuse and threats and injured all the rest of her servants.

36. POSEIDON*

*otherwise unknown

1. It is difficult to relate the many things that are known of Poseidon of Thebes: how meek he was,

how extremely spiritually disciplined, how utterly without guile—I do not know if I ever met such a one. I lived with this man in Bethlehem for a year while he was accommodated beyond the Shepherds' Field,* and I witnessed his many virtues.

*see Luke 2:8

2. Among other things he told me this himself one day: "I lived a year in the region of Porphyrites* and did not meet a single man all the year long; I heard no conversation and partook of no bread. I existed on small dates and wild herbs if I found any. On one occasion, for lack of food, I came out of the cave to go to the habited world,

*see *Lausiac History* 34.3

3. "and in spite of walking all day long, I got scarcely two miles from the cave. I looked around and saw a man on horseback who appeared to be a soldier with a tiara-like helmet on his head. Expecting that he was a soldier, I hastened as far as the cave and found a basket of fresh grapes and figs. This I received with great joy and went into the cave; the consolation of those edibles lasted me for two months."

4. He performed this miracle in Bethlehem: a pregnant woman had an unclean spirit, and she was having difficulty at the time of giving birth since the spirit was tormenting her. As the woman was in the power of a demon, her husband appeared and begged that holy man to come. We went in together to pray. He stood in prayer and, after the second genuflexion, threw out the spirit.

5. He stood up and said to us, "Pray, for now he is driving out the unclean spirit, but there has to be a sign so we may be assured." And as the demon was coming out, he threw down the entire wall of the courtyard right to its foundations. The woman

had not spoken for six years, but after the demon went out, she gave birth and spoke.

6. I became aware of this prophecy by that man Poseidon: a priest named Jerome[20] was living in those parts, distinguished by his command of Latin literature and cleverness, but he was so jealous that his jealousy obscured his literary skill. Poseidon (who had stayed with him for quite a number of days) said in my ear, "I think the noble Paula who looks after him will die before he does, to relieve herself of his jealousy.

7. "Because of this man no holy man will inhabit those parts, for his envy will extend even to his own brother." That was what in fact happened: Jerome drove out Oxyperentius, the blessed Italian, and some Egyptian named Peter, and Symeon, wondrous men whom I myself observed for a while. This Poseidon told me that in forty years he had never tasted bread or held a grudge against anybody for half a day.

37. SERAPION SINDONIOS

1. There was another Serapion[21] known as *sindonios* because he never wore anything other

[20] Palladius makes little attempt to hide his antipathy to Jerome (ca. 342–420), who accused him of Origenism in his *Dialogue against the Pelagians* (Prologue 2).

[21] Several Egyptian monks of this name are known: Serapion the Great of Nitria (*Lausiac History* 7.3), Serapion of Arsinoe (Monks 18), and some monks of Scete mentioned by Cassian (Conf 2.10, 11; Conf 5; Conf 10.3.1; and Conf 18.11.2, the last being the Serapion of whom four sayings are recorded in APalph, PG 65:413D–417A. Serapion *sindonios* (see also APanon 565, 566; APsys 15.116, 117) is none of the above.

*sindôn

than a sheet.* He was greatly disciplined in indifference to possessions, and, being highly literate, he learned all the Scriptures by heart. What with his utter indifference to possessions and his meditation on the Scriptures he was unable to remain calmly in a cell. Not that he was distracted by material goods, for he achieved this virtue going around the inhabited world. That was his nature, for there are differences of nature but not of substance.

2. The fathers used to tell that he took a monk as companion and sold himself to some Greek actors in a city for twenty pieces of gold, then sealed up the pieces of gold and kept them on his person. He stayed with the actors who had bought him and served them until he made them Christians and separated them from the theater, partaking of nothing other than bread and water and not silencing his mouth from meditating* the Scriptures.

*i.e., reciting, usually aloud

3. In the process of time, first the leading actor was pricked in his conscience, and then the actress who was his wife, then their entire company. It was said that for as long as they were in ignorance of him he used to wash all their feet. So when both had been baptized they gave up the theater and, embarking on a decent and devout way of life, greatly revered the man. They said to him, "Come, brother, let us set you free since it is you who set us free from our shameful servitude." He said to them, "Since God took the initiative and your soul was saved, let me tell you the secret of what has taken place.

4. "I, an Egyptian free man and a monk, took pity on your soul. For that reason I sold myself in order to save you. Since God has done it and your

soul has been saved through my humility, take your gold so I can go away and help other people." They greatly besought him and affirmed, "We will have you as our father, as our lord-and-master, only stay with us!" But they could not persuade him. Then they said to him, "Give the gold to the poor, for it has become a foretaste of salvation for us, but you come and see us at least once a year."

5. In the course of his frequent journeys this Serapion came to Greece. Three days he stayed in Athens and was not deemed worthy of bread by any man. He was carrying no money, no pouch, no sheepskin cloak, nothing like that. When the fourth day broke he became very hungry; involuntary hunger is dreadful when it is accompanied by a lack of faith. Standing on an eminence of the city where the city authorities used to assemble,[22] he began to lament bitterly, clapping his hands and crying, "Men of Athens, help!"

6. Everybody came running toward him, philosophers and ordinary citizens, saying, "What is the matter? Where are you from? Are you in pain?" He told them, "I am an Egyptian by birth. I have fallen foul of three moneylenders since I left my true fatherland. Two of them have departed from me, for, after being paid what was owing, they had no more claim on me, but the one does not depart from me." Inquiring diligently about the moneylenders (in order to satisfy their curiosity), those people asked him, "Where are they and who are they? Who is the one who is harassing you? Show him to us so we may help you."

[22] Presumably the Areopagus; see Acts 17:19-34.

7. Then he said to them, "From my youth up the love of money, gluttony, and *porneia*—they harass me. I have been relieved of two of them, the love of money and *porneia*—they harass me no longer—but I am unable to be relieved of love of food. This is the fourth day I have not eaten, and my belly keeps on harassing me, seeking its customary payment, without which I am unable to live." Then some of the philosophers, suspecting that he was putting on an act, gave him a piece of gold; he accepted it and set it down in a bread shop. He took one loaf and then promptly made off, traveling away from the city, and he never came back to it.

8. Then the philosophers perceived that he was indeed a man of virtue; they gave the breadseller the price of the loaf and took the piece of gold. When Serapion came into the area around Sparta, he heard that one of the leading citizens was a Manichee, he and all his household, but that in other respects he was a man of virtue. To this man he sold himself again, as in the first instance and, within two years, had detached this man and his good wife from the heresy and brought them to the church. Then they loved him and no longer treated him as a slave but as a dear brother or father—and they were glorifying God.

9. This man once got himself on board a ship as one who needed to sail to Rome. Thinking that he had either already paid his fare or that he had the cost in gold about him, the sailors simply accepted him, each thinking that somebody else had handled his baggage. As they sailed away and were about five hundred furlongs* from Alexandria, just

*ca. 100 km.

as the sun was setting, the passengers began to eat (the sailors had eaten earlier).

10. They saw that Serapion was not eating the first day and thought it was because of the sailing; it was the same on the second day, on the third, and on the fourth. On the fifth day, seeing him sitting still while they were all eating, they said to him, "Fellow, why are you not eating?" He told them, "Because I do not have anything." So they inquired of each other, "Who handled his baggage or took his fare?"

11. When they found that nobody had, they began to contend with him, saying, "How come you embarked without the fare? Where are you going to get the passage money from to give us? How are you going to feed yourself?" He told them, "In fact, I do not have anything. Take me and toss me where you found me." But not even for a hundred pieces of gold would they divert: they just continued toward their destination. Thus he was in the ship, and they found themselves feeding him all the way to Rome.

12. When he got to Rome he inquired whether there was a great practitioner of spiritual discipline, male or female, in the city. Among them he also met one Domninus, a disciple of Origen, whose bed healed the sick after he died. As he met with Domninus and benefited from the occasion (for this was a man well rounded in both character and knowledge), he inquired of him who else there might be, male or female, and he was made aware of a spinster living in *hesychia* who would not meet anybody.

13. He found out where she was living, then went and said to the old woman who looked after

her, "Tell the spinster, 'It is essential that I meet you, for God sent me.'" He waited for two or three days and finally met her. He said to her, "Why are you still?" "I am not still; I am traveling," she told him, and he said to her, "Where are you traveling to?" She said, "Toward God." He said to her, "Are you alive, or have you died?" She said to him, "I trust in God that I have died, for the person who is alive in the flesh will not be traveling." He said to her, "Do then what I do to assure me that you have died," and she said to him, "Charge me with something possible and I will do it."

14. He answered her, "Everything is possible for a dead person except sacrilege." The he said to her, "Come out and go," but she answered him, "I have not gone out for twenty-five years; why should I go out?" He said to her, "If you have died to the world and the world is dead to you, it is all the same to you whether you go out or not, so go out." Out she went, and after she had gone out she came to some church. Inside the church he said to her, "If you want to assure me that you have died and that you are no longer living and pleasing men, do what I do; then I will know that you have died.

15. "Take off all your clothes (as I am doing); put them on your shoulders and pass through the city center, with me going before you in the same guise." She said to him, "I will give offense to many people by the unseemliness of my behavior, and they could say, 'She is out of her mind and demon possessed.'" He answered her, "And what do you care if they say, 'She is out of her mind and demon possessed'? You have died to them." Then that woman said to

him: "I will do anything else you desire, but I do not even pray to measure up to that."

16. Then he said to her, "See then that you no longer think so highly of yourself as more pious than everybody else and as having died to the world. For I am more dead than you are, and I show by my action that I have died to the world, for I do this insensibly and shamelessly." He then left her reduced to humility; having shattered her conceit he went his way. But there are many other wondrous works[23] he has accomplished tending

[23] Compare APanon 565 and 566, APsys 15.116 and 117: They used to say of Abba Serapion that, such was his life, it was like that of one of the birds. Not a thing of this world did he possess, nor did he ever stay in a cell. He used to go around with a little gospel wearing a shroud, like an incorporeal being. They would often find him sitting outside a village or by the roadside, weeping bitterly. When he was asked, "Why are you crying like that, elder?" he replied, "My lord-and-master entrusted me with his wealth, but I have lost and squandered it; he wants to punish and to lose me." Thinking he was talking about money, they who were hearing this threw him a little bread, saying, "Take this, brother, and, so far as the wealth you lost, God can send it to you," to which the elder answered, "Amen."

Another time when he was going around in Alexandria he met a pauper shivering with cold. Coming to a standstill, he thought to himself, "How can I, who am supposed to be an ascetic and a worker, be wearing a smock while this pauper (or rather, Christ himself)* is dying of cold? If I leave him to die, I shall certainly be judged to be a murderer on the Day of Judgment." Stripping down like a good athlete, he gave the article of clothing he was wearing to the pauper. Then he sat down naked with the little gospel he always carried tucked under his arm. When the so-called peace officer came by and saw him naked, he said to him, "Abba Serapion, who stripped you?" Producing the little gospel, he said to him, "This one stripped me." Getting up from there, he met another person who was being arrested for debt by somebody else and could not repay. This immortal Serapion sold the gospel and gave

*Matt 25:35-45

toward *apatheia*. He died in the sixtieth year of his life and was buried in Rome itself.

38. EVAGRIUS PONTICUS[24]

1. It would be unjust to remain silent concerning the ever-memorable deacon Evagrius, a man who lived like one of the apostles. So, counting it worthwhile to set it down in writing for the edification of those who encounter it and for the glory of the goodness of our Savior, I will start at the beginning: how he attained his objective and how, having worthily practiced it, he died in the desert fifty-four years old, as it is written, "He fulfilled
Wis 4:13 many years in a short time."

2. He was a man of Pontus by birth, from the city of Ibora, the son of a rural bishop. He had been ordained a lector by the holy Basil, bishop of the
379 church of Caesarea. After the holy Basil died, the most wise, the most devoid of passion and brilliant in learning Gregory, bishop of Nazianzen, noted his suitability and ordained him deacon. Then, at

---

toward the debt of the poor man who was suffering violence; then off he went, naked, to his cell. When his disciple saw him naked, he said to him, "Abba, where is your little vest?" The elder told him, "I sent it on to where we shall need it, my son." "And where is the little gospel?" the brother said to him. The elder replied, "Well, naturally my son, that being the very thing that says to me every day, 'Sell all that you have and give to the
Matt 19:21 poor,' I sold it and gave away the proceeds so that we shall enjoy greater familiarity with him on the Day of Judgment."

[24] Evagrius (346–399) himself, once having been a disciple of Macarius the Egyptian and Macarius of Alexandria (*Lausiac History* 17, 18) was Palladius's abba. From 382 he lived first in the Desert of Nitria, then at The Cells.

the great synod in Constantinople,* he left him with the blessed Bishop Nectarius* as one who was most skilled in dialectic against all the heresies. Evagrius flourished in the great city, inveighing against every heresy with hot-headed homilies.

*381

*archbishop of Constantinople 381–397

3. While he was highly honored by the entire city, it came about that he was fixated by the chimera of desire for a woman, as he told us himself later when his mind had been liberated. The woman returned his love too, and she was of the nobility. But Evagrius feared God and respected his own conscience. Setting before his eyes the magnitude of the disgrace and the malignant joy it would give the heretics, he prayed to God, begging that he might be impeded by him. But the woman was persistent and fervent; he wanted to get away from her, but he had not the strength, for he was detained by the bonds of her attention to him.

4. Not long after, his prayer having prospered before he had experienced the act, there appeared to him an angelic vision in the form of soldiers of the governor. They arrested him and took him as though into a courthouse, throwing him into what they call the guard house, having bound his neck and hands with iron rings and chains. They who came for him did not tell the reason, but in his conscience he himself knew that he was undergoing these things on her account, and he anticipated a confrontation with her husband.

5. While he was so severely distressed, another case was proceeding and others were being tortured on some charge. He continued to be greatly distressed, but the angel who had provided the vision transformed himself into the appearance of a

true friend and said to him, who was now bound in the middle of a file of forty of the accused, "Deacon, for what reason are you being held here, sir?" He said to him, "I honestly do not know, but I have a suspicion that, smitten by an unreasonable jealousy, so-and-so the ex-governor entered a plea against me, and I am afraid that, bribed with money, the magistrate will subject me to retribution."

6. He said to him, "If you will listen to your friend, it is not to your advantage to stay in this city." Evagrius said to him, "If God releases me from this misfortune and you see me in Constantinople, be sure that I am undergoing this punishment for good reason." The other said to him, "I am carrying the gospel; swear to me upon it that you will withdraw from this city and will look after your soul, and I will release you from this constraint."

7. Taking the gospel, he swore to him on it, "But for one day so I can stow my clothes aboard ship, I will not stay." After the oath was pronounced, he came back out of the ecstasy that had happened to him in the night. He got up and thought to himself, "Even though the oath took place in an ecstasy, nevertheless I did swear," so he put all he owned aboard ship and came to Jerusalem,

8. and there he was received by the blessed Melania of Rome. Again the devil hardened his heart, as he did Pharaoh's.* Being a young man in the prime of life, he began to have doubts and to be of two minds, but he said nothing to anybody. From there he went on to changing his clothes again, and vainglory began to stupefy him in his debating. But God, who impedes the destruction of us all,

*Exod 4:21, etc.

threw him into a chance fever and, subsequently, into a long illness that wasted his flesh and incapacitated him for six months.

9. The physicians were at a loss, for they found no way of healing him. The blessed Melania said to him, "Son, I do not like this protracted illness of yours, so tell me what is on your mind, for this illness of yours is not from God." He then confessed the whole matter to her. She said to him, "Give me your word before the Lord that you aim to embrace the monastic life and, sinner though I be, I will pray that an extension of life be given to you." He agreed, and within a few days he recovered. When he got up he was reclothed* by Melania herself; then he went out, departing to the Mountain of Nitria in Egypt.

*i.e., with the monastic habit

10. He lived there for two years; in the third year he ventured into the desert. He lived fourteen years at what is called The Cells, eating a pound of bread each day and one *sextarius** of olive oil in three months, this man who had been leading a life of extreme luxury, daintiness, and comfort. He used to offer a hundred prayers and, working as a scribe, earned in a year only the price of what he ate. He was naturally suited to writing the sharp-pointed letters.* Having purged his mind to the limit for fifteen years, he was deemed worthy of the spiritual gift of knowledge, of wisdom, and of the discernment of spirits. He composed three sacred books for monks called *Refutations*, setting out methods of countering the demons.

*567 cc.

*meaning unknown; probably "a fine hand"

11. The demon of *porneia* was particularly hard on him (as he told us himself). He stood naked in the well all night long in wintertime so that his

flesh froze. Another time the spirit of blasphemy troubled him; as he told us, for forty days he did not come in under a roof, so that ticks devoured his body as they do those of animals with no reason. Three demons presented themselves to him in one day disguised as clergy, inquiring about the faith. One said he was an Arian, one a Eunomian, and one an Apollinarian. In his wisdom he quickly got the better of them with a few words.

12. Then again another day, when the church key was lost he made the sign of the cross on the face of the locking device, pushed with his hand, and opened [the door] after he had called on Christ. This man was so scourged by demons and subject to such trials by demons that there is no numbering them. He told one of his disciples what was going to happen to him eighteen years later, prophesying in detail everything to him. He used to say, "Ever since I came to live in the desert I have taken neither lettuce nor any other green vegetable; no fruit, no grapes, no meat—not even a bath."

13. Later on, in the sixteenth year of this way of life without cooked food, on account of a malady of the stomach, his flesh needed to partake of something cooked. He still would not take bread, but partaking of barley water and little pulses for two years and existing on this, he died at Epiphany after making his Communion in the church. He affirmed {to us} when he lay dying, "This is the third year that I have not been troubled by carnal desire after such a life, so much labor and toil, so much continuous prayer." When the death of his father was reported to him, he said to the one who told him of it, "Stop blaspheming, for my father is immortal."

39. PIÔR[25]

1. Piôr, an Egyptian, renounced the world as a young man and left his father's house, giving his word to God (through an excess of zeal) never again to set eyes on one of his own people. Fifty years later his sister, who had grown old, heard that he was alive, and she was approaching a state of distraction unless she could see him. As she could not go into the great desert, she besought the bishop of the region to write to the fathers in the desert to send him so she might see him. After much coercion had been applied to Piôr, he decided to take another and go,

2. and at the house of the sister someone indicated, "Your brother Piôr is here." Standing outside, he perceived from the noise of the door (for he had closed his eyes) that the old lady had come out to meet him; he called out: "Oh N . . . , oh N . . . ! I am your brother Piôr, it is indeed I: look at me as much as you like." She was convinced and glorified God, but, unable to persuade him to enter her house, she returned into her own house. But Piôr offered a prayer at the doorposts, then removed himself into the desert again.

3. This wonder is attributed to him: he dug and found water that was very bitter in the place where he lived. He stayed there until he died, satisfied with the bitterness, to demonstrate his own patient

[25] Piôr (d. ca. 360) has already been mentioned (*Lausiac History* 10.8). "Every day he made a new start" (Poemen 83, PG 65:341C). When he was very young he became a monk with Antony, who sent him to live alone between Scete and Nitria, where he stayed for many years. Three apophthegms are attributed to Piôr in APalph, PG 65:373B–376A.

endurance. Many monks competed to stay in his cell after he died but were unable to last a year, for the place is terrifying and comfortless.

4. Moses the Libyan, a most gentle and affectionate man, was deemed worthy of the spiritual gift of healing. This man told me, "We dug a very large well at the monastery where I was in my youth, twenty feet wide. For three days eighty men excavated it and went a cubit beyond the level at which a spring is usually expected, but we did not find water. We were very disappointed and were thinking of abandoning the project. Then out of the great desert there came Piôr just at the sixth hour, in the burning heat, an old man wearing his sheepskin cloak. He greeted us; then, after the greeting, he said, 'Why did you get discouraged, you of little faith? For I have seen you discouraged since yesterday.'

5. "Going down into the excavation for the well by the ladder, he offered a prayer together with those who were digging. Then he took the mattock and, striking the third blow, said, 'O God of the holy patriarchs, let not the labor of your servants be in vain, but send them the water they need.' And right away water sprang up: they were all sprinkled. He prayed again, and then he was going home. They constrained him to eat, but he would not agree, saying, 'What I was sent to do is done; I was not sent for that.'"

40. EPHRAIM[26]

1. You have certainly heard about Ephraim, deacon of the church at Edessa, for he was one of those among the saints who deserves to be commemorated. When he had duly traveled the path of the Spirit without digressing from the straight way, he was deemed worthy of the spiritual gift of natural knowledge, succeeded by theology and utter blessedness. He always led a spiritually disciplined life of *hesychia*, for many years edifying those who visited him, but eventually he left his cell for the following reason.

2. A severe famine was affecting the city of Edessa. Filled with compassion for the entire agricultural community that was perishing, he went to those who were well provided with means and said to them, "Why do you not take pity on the human nature that is perishing instead of wasting your wealth to the condemnation of your souls?" They thought about this question, then said to him, "There is nobody we will trust to be of service to the famished; they all traffic in the goods." He said to them, "What do you think of me?" He had a great reputation (a genuine one, not false) with everybody.

3. They said to him: "We know you are a man of God." "Trust me then," he said. "Look, through you I am appointing myself guestmaster." Taking their money, he subdivided the porticoes, installed about three hundred beds, and began caring for

[26] Ephraim Syrus (ca. 306–373), a deacon at Nisibis who moved to Edessa in 363, was a highly prolific writer in Syriac of poetry and prose. See Sozomen, HE 3.16.

the famished. He buried those who died and cared for those who had a hope of living. In brief, using the resources with which he had been furnished, he provided hospitality and care on a daily basis for all those who came that way on account of the famine.

4. When the year was out, abundance had followed, and everybody went home. As he had nothing to do anymore, he went into his own cell and died a month later; God had conceded him this initiative in the form of a crown at the end of his life. He left compositions of which the majority are worth studying.

41. HOLY WOMEN

1. In this book I must also commemorate some courageous women whom God granted equality in prizes with men so as not to allege that they are less vigorous in the quest for virtue. I have seen many of them and met many sophisticated spinsters and widows,

2. {among whom was Paula the Roman, the mother of Toxotius, a woman greatly advanced in her spiritual way of life. A certain Jerome from Dalmatia became a stumbling block for her. She was capable of flying higher than everybody, for she was very talented, but in his jealousy he stood in her way, having won her over to his own point of view. It is her daughter—Eustochio [*sic*] by name—who is now practicing spiritual discipline in Bethlehem. I have not had a meeting with her, but she is said to be a woman of extreme discretion, having a community of fifty spinsters.

3. I also made the acquaintance of Veneria, the wife of Count Vallovicus, who had generously distributed the camel's load[27] and delivered herself from the wounds of material possessions. Also of Theodora, the tribune's wife, who became so indifferent to possessions that she had to accept charity, and so she died in the Hesycha monastery by the sea. I made the acquaintance of one Hosia, a most venerable woman in every respect, and of her sister, Adolia, who was not her equal but lived according to her own ability.

4. I also made the acquaintance of Basianilla, wife of Candidianus the general, who fervently and devoutly espoused the disciplined pursuit of virtue and is still even now heavily engaged in fighting the good fight. Also of the utterly venerable spinster Phôteinê, the daughter of Theoctistus the priest at Laodicea, and in Antioch I encountered a most venerable woman who speaks with God, the deaconess Savinianê, the aunt of John [Chrysostom], the bishop of Constantinople. At Rome I also saw the good Asella, the spinster who had grown old in the monastery, a most gentle woman, quite content with community life.

5. Among these I saw men and women recently catechized. I also saw Abita "worthy of God" together with Apronianus her husband and their daughter Eunomia, all three being well pleasing to God to the point of openly converting to the virtuous and continent way of life, and so they were deemed worthy of falling asleep in Christ,

[27] Apparently her worldly wealth; *une partie de ses biens*, suggests one translator; *il carico del suo cammello* another. See Matt 19:24.

liberated from all sin and participating in knowledge, having abandoned their life, [leaving behind] a good reminiscence.}

42. JULIAN OF EDESSA

{I have heard of one Julian near the city of Edessa, a man utterly devoted to spiritual discipline, who so excessively reduced his body that he consisted only of skin and bone. Toward the end of his life he was deemed worthy of the honor of the spiritual gift of healing.}

43. ADOLIOS

1. I made the acquaintance of somebody back in Jerusalem called Adolios, a man of Tarsus who, once he arrived in Jerusalem, seriously traveled the untraveled way, not the one that many of us took, but cutting out a strange way of life for himself. His spiritual discipline was beyond human endurance, so that the demons themselves trembled at his austerity and dared not approach him. His abstinence and wakefulness were so excessive that he was suspected of being a mere phantom.

2. In Lent he ate every five days, the rest of the time every second day. His great activity was this: from evening until when the brotherhood assembled again in the houses of prayer, he spent the time standing at the place of the Ascension (from which Jesus was taken up) on the Mount of Olives, singing and praying. Whether it snowed or rained or froze, there he remained, unmoved.

3. When he had completed his usual span he would knock at the cells of them all with the wake-up hammer, congregating them in the houses of prayer. He would sing the first or second antiphon along with them in each house, and, praying along with them, in that manner he would go to his own cell before daybreak—often in such a state (this is the truth) that the brothers took the clothes off him, wrung them out as if they had been washed, and put others on him. He would repose himself until the time for psalm singing, in which he would engage himself until evening. And that then is the virtue of Adolios of Tarsus, who died at Jerusalem and was buried there.

44. INNOCENT[28]

1. While you have heard from many folk about the blessed Innocent, priest at the [Mount of] Olives, you will hear no less from us who lived with him for three years. He was a man of extraordinary simplicity. He was one of the palace grandees at the beginning of the reign of the emperor Constantius;* then he renounced the world, starting with *337–361
his marriage, from which he had a son named Paul (serving in the army as a domestic), who

2. had sinned against a priest's daughter. Innocent cursed his own son, praying to God and saying, "Lord, give him such a spirit that he will never again find occasion to sin in the flesh," thinking it better for him to fight with a demon than with a

[28] On the possibility that this might be the future Pope Innocent I (402–417), see Butler, 2:219–20, n80.

licentious nature, and that was what happened. The son is still even now on the Mount of Olives in irons, chastised by the spirit.

3. I shall seem silly if I tell the truth about how compassionate this Innocent was, how he often stole from the brothers and gave to the needy. He was totally without guile and straightforward; he was deemed worthy of the spiritual gift against demons. For example, once there was brought to him, with us looking on, a youth, prey to a spirit and paralysis, so that I, when I saw him, immediately wanted to send away the mother who had brought him, since I despaired of a cure.

4. Now meanwhile, as it happened, the elder came by and saw her standing there weeping and lamenting over the indescribable misfortune of her son. Weeping himself and torn with compassion, the good elder took the youth and went into his own *martyrium*, which he had built himself, wherein lay relics of John the Baptist. He prayed for him from the third to the ninth hour, then the same day gave the youth back to his mother, cured. He had driven out the demon and his paralysis. (His paralysis had been such that if he spat, he spat on his own back, he was so distorted.)

5. An old woman who had lost a sheep came crying to him. He followed her, saying, "Show me the place where you lost it." She led him to the region around the Lazarium,* and he stood praying. Now the lads who had stolen it had gone so far as to slaughter it. While he was praying nobody confessed. Now the carcass was hidden in the vineyard; from somewhere a crow came and alighted on it, seized a morsel, and flew off again.

*a church at Bethany marking the spot where Lazarus was raised, John 11

The blessed man took heed and found the meat, and so the lads who had slaughtered it fell before him and confessed; they were required to pay the due cost.

45. PHILOROMOS

1. {In Galatia we met and spent a lot of time with the priest Philoromos, highly disciplined spiritually and capable of the greatest endurance. His mother was a slave, the father a free man. He demonstrated such graciousness in his Christian way of life that even those unbeatable in their bloodline stood in awe of his life and virtue. He had renounced the world in the days of the ill-omened emperor Julian, with whom he would speak without restraint. Julian had commanded him to be shaved and punched by some youths. He endured the experience and expressed his thanks to Julian, as he told us himself.

2. *Porneia* and gluttony declared bitter war on him at the beginning, but he drove the passion off by imprisoning himself, wearing irons, and abstaining from bread made from wheat and everything that had been cooked with fire. When he had endured these conditions for eighteen years he sang the hymn of victory to Christ. Variously embattled by the spirits of wickedness, he persevered in one monastery for forty years. He affirmed, "For thirty-two years I never touched any fruit." He was once embattled by fear and sequestered himself in a tomb for six years to overcome it.

3. The blessed Bishop Basil was greatly concerned for Philoromos, well pleased at his austerity

and restraint. Even to this day, eighty years old, he has not laid aside pen and quarto for writing. He said, "Since I was catechized and born again until this present day I never ate the gift of another's bread: only what came from my own labors." With God as his witness he convinced us that he had donated to the mutilated two hundred and fifty pieces of gold [earned by] the work of his hands and that he had never treated anybody unjustly.

4. He made the journey on foot as far as Rome itself to pray at the *martyrium* of the blessed Peter. He got as far as Alexandria to pray at the *martyrium* of Mark. He came to Jerusalem a second time, traveling on his own feet and paying his own expenses. He used to say, "I do not recollect ever having been separated in my mind from my God."}

46. MELANIA THE ELDER

1. The thrice-blessed Melania was a Spaniard by birth, hence a Roman. She was a daughter of the consul Marcellinus* and the wife of some high-ranking man whom I do not remember well. After being widowed at twenty-two, she was deemed worthy of divine love, and, in the times when Valens* was ruling the Empire, without a word to anybody (for she would have been prevented), she arranged for a guardian to be appointed for her son, and, taking all her movable property, she put it on board a ship. Then together with some designated slaves and women she took a hasty passage to Alexandria.

*Melania (325–410) appears to have been the granddaughter of Antony Marcellinus, consul in 341

*364–378

2. There, after she had sold her goods and turned it into gold coins, she went to the Mount

of Nitria, where she met the fathers, those with Pambô, Arsisios, Serapion the Great, Paphnoutius of Scete, Isidore the confessor and bishop of Hermoupolis, and Dioscorus. She spent up to half a year with them, traveling around in the desert, investigating all the holy ones.

3. Subsequently the prefect of Alexandria exiled Isidore, Pisimius, Adelphius, Paphnoutius, and Pambô to the region of Diocaesarea in Palestine, together with Ammonius the one-eared[29] plus twelve bishops and priests. These she followed and supported with her own resources. According to what they said, they were debarred from having servants (for I met the holy Pisimius, Isidore, Paphnoutius, and Ammonius), so she herself put on slave's attire and brought them what they needed in the evenings. When the consul of Palestine became aware of this, he expected that he could blackmail her, wishing to fill his pockets.

4. He arrested her and threw her into jail, unaware that she was a free woman, but she declared before him, "I am the daughter of N . . . , the widow of N . . . , and the servant of Christ; do not despise the meanness of my appearance. I am capable of raising myself up if I want to; you cannot terrify me in this matter or take what is mine. This I revealed to you so you do not unwittingly incur charges. Like a falcon, one has to make use of pride against the insensitive." Grasping the situation, the magistrate apologized, paid her due respect, and ordered that she have unimpeded access to the holy ones.

[29] See *Lausiac History* 7.1.

5. After they were recalled, she built a monastery at Jerusalem and passed twenty-seven years there, where she had a community of fifty spinsters. Rufinus* from the city of Aquileia in Italy was living there too, a most noble person with a similar lifestyle and enormous strength who was subsequently deemed worthy of the priesthood; none is to be found among men who was more knowledgeable and modest.

*340/345–410

6. For twenty-seven years they both received as their guests persons visiting Jerusalem to pray: bishops, monks, and spinsters. They accommodated all who visited at their own expense. They healed the schism concerning Paulinus (about four hundred monks), and every heretic at odds with the Spirit they jointly persuaded and led into the church. They honored the local clergy with gifts and sustenance; thus they ran their course without offending anybody.

47. CHRONIUS AND PAPHNOUTIUS

1. [A person] named Chronius* from the village called Phoenike* measured five thousand double paces away from his own village (which was adjacent to the desert), and there he prayed, then dug a well. When he found excellent water seven fathoms* down, he built himself a small dwelling there. From the day he installed himself in that monastery he prayed to God that he would never again remove to an inhabited place.

*not to be confused with Cronius, the priest of Nitria, *Lausiac History* 21

*location unknown

*ca. 13 m.

2. A few years went by, and he was deemed worthy to be the priest for the brotherhood of about two hundred men that had been gathered around him.

This virtue of his spiritual discipline is reported: he served at the altar as a priest for sixty years without leaving the desert; nor did he eat bread that was not earned by the labor of his hands. Living with him there was one Jacob from somewhere nearby, a man of exceptional learning, known as "the lame." Both men were known to the blessed Antony.

3. One day Paphnoutius,[30] known as Cephalas, hastened to join them; he had the spiritual gift of knowledge of the Sacred Scriptures, the Old and the New Testaments; he interpreted it all without having read the Scriptures. He was so modest that he concealed his prophetic virtue; it is reported of him that in eighty years he did not possess two tunics at a time. When those blessed men Evagrius and Alban and I met them we sought to discover the reasons that brothers fall by the wayside, or even fall into error or do wrong in a life that is as it should be.

4. It happened at about that time that Chairemon the solitary died sitting up; he was found dead in his chair holding his work in his hands. It also happened that another brother who was digging a well was buried by the well, while another died for lack of water, coming from Scete. Then too there is the case of Stephen, who fell into shameful profligacy, of Eucarpius, of Hero of Alexandria, of Valens of Palestine, and of Ptolemy the Egyptian at Scete.

[30] There are five sayings of Paphnoutios Cephalas in APalph (PG 65:377C–380D) and several references to him, e.g., in the twenty-ninth saying attributed to Antony the Great ("Here is a man indeed, capable of healing and saving souls," PG 65:85AB) and elsewhere. Cassian visited Paphnoutios when he was ninety (Conf 3).

5. So we were inquiring what the reason might be why some men living like that in the wilderness were led astray in the mind while others broke out in licentiousness. Paphnoutius (that most-knowledgeable one) gave us this answer: "All the things that happen are divided into two: what is well pleasing to God and what he permits. So then, whatever is done virtuously and to the glory of God, that is well pleasing to God. But everything that is hurtful, dangerous, precarious, and improper comes about by divine permission.

6. "Permission is according to reason, for it is impossible for one who thinks and lives uprightly to fall into shameful errors or those of demonic deceit. So they who appear to seek after virtue but have a perverse goal (e.g., the sickness of pleasing men or the stubborn assertion of their own thoughts), they too fall into mistakes, and God abandons them for their own benefit so that through the abandonment, perceiving the difference, as a result of the change they set right either their intention or their action.

7. "For sometimes the intention is sinful, for example when it takes place with evil intent, and sometimes the action, for example when it is performed in a corrupt way or not in the way it ought to be performed, with corrupt intent. This often happens when the licentious person gives alms to a young woman with perverse intent and a shameful end in view, but it is a blessed deed to give succor to a woman who is an orphan, a solitary, or one under spiritual discipline. It happens too that one gives alms with an upright intent to the sick, the aged, and those who have lost their fortune, albeit

in a niggardly manner and resentfully—then the intention is upright, the action unworthy of the intention. For the almsgiver must be compassionate joyfully and generously."

8. They would also say, "There are excellences in many souls: in some a clearness of mind, in others an aptitude for spiritual discipline. But when neither the action nor the cleverness comes about because of that which is good, and those who possess excellences do not ascribe them to God, the giver of good things, but to their own motive, cleverness, and sufficiency, then such people are abandoned or caught up in shameful deeds or submission to obscenity and shame; they gradually cleanse themselves somehow of the conceit in what they supposed to be virtue.

9. "When one who is puffed up and exults in his cleverness with words ascribes neither his cleverness nor his supply of knowledge to God but to his own spiritual discipline or nature, God takes the angel of providence away. When that angel has been taken away, the one who exalts himself for cleverness, oppressed by the enemy, falls into licentiousness on account of pride, so that (since the witness to continence has been taken away) whatever he says is unworthy of belief. The godly themselves flee from the teaching that comes out of such a mouth, as from a well with leeches in it, in fulfilment of that which is written: 'God says to the sinner, "Why do you recite my judgments and take my covenant in your mouth?"'* *Ps 49:16

10. "The souls of the impassioned indeed resemble various types of wells. The gluttonous and the winebibbers are like muddied wells,

those devoted to money and the covetous are like wells with frogs in them, and slanderers and arrogant people who have facility in learning are like wells that nourish serpents, in which the discourse always forms stagnant pools but nobody gladly draws from them on account of the bitterness of their character. Hence David begged, asking for three things, 'Goodness, discipline, and knowledge,'* for knowledge without goodness is useless.

*Ps 118:66

11. "And if such a person straightens himself out, setting aside the reason for his abandonment (meaning conceit), if he becomes humble minded and aware of his own limits, not exalting himself over anyone and giving thanks to God, attested knowledge will come upon him again. Spiritual discourses that are not accompanied by a decent and temperate life are windblown ears of grain: they have the appearance but lack the nutrition.

12. "Every falling into sin, whether occasioned by tongue, by feelings, by deed, or by the entire body, comes about by divine permission, and God has consideration for those who are being abandoned. For if with their licentiousness the Lord also bears witness to their cleverness by furnishing them with fine words, pride renders them demons as they exalt themselves in their impurity."

13. Those men also said these things to us: "When you see somebody whose life is harmful but speech persuasive, be mindful of the demon who speaks to Christ in Holy Scripture and of the text that says, 'Now the serpent was most subtle of all the beasts on earth'*—or rather his intellect was, for it became its harm since no other virtue accompanied it in its

*Gen 3:1

case. The faithful and good person must think the thoughts that God supplies, speak what God thinks, and do what God says.

14. "For if there is no connection operating between one's life and the truth of one's words, it is bread without salt (as Job says), which is either not eaten at all or, if it is eaten, will bring those who eat it to a bad condition. 'Shall bread be eaten without salt?' he says, 'and is there any taste in empty words' that are not fulfilled by the witness of deeds?* The reasons for abandonment are these: *Job 6:6
one is that hidden virtue might be brought to light, as in the case of Job when God has dealings with him and says, 'Do not deny my judgment; do not think I have had dealings with you other than that you might appear righteous,* *Job 40:3

15. "'for you were known to me who see the hidden things, and, when you were unknown to men and they thought you were serving me for riches, I brought disaster and cut away your wealth to show them your grateful disposition.' Another [cause for abandonment] is to eliminate pride, as in the case of Paul. For Paul was abandoned and thrown into all sorts of calamities, beatings, and afflictions, and he said, 'There was given to me a thorn in the flesh, an angel of Satan to buffet me to prevent me from becoming overbearing.'* *2 Cor 12:7

16. "Maybe the wonders, ease, success, and honor accorded him would have cast him into conceit and diabolical vanity. The paralyzed person was abandoned on account of sin, as Jesus says, 'See, you have become whole; sin no more.' Judas was abandoned because he valued money above the word, wherefore he hanged himself.

Esau was abandoned and fell into licentiousness for preferring the filth of the entrails to his father's blessing.

17. "So it is that, aware of all this, Paul says of certain folk, 'Since they did not resolve to have a knowledge of God, God handed them over to their discredited mind to do what was unseemly.' Concerning others who seem to have knowledge of God with a corrupt mind, 'Since they know God but do not glorify him or give thanks to him as God, God has given them over to shameful passions.'* From this we know that it is impossible for a person to fall into licentiousness unless abandoned by the providence of God."

*Rom 1:27

48. ELPIDIUS

1. Down from Jericho there are the caves of the Amorites that they had excavated when they were fleeing from Joshua the son of Nun, who was then pillaging the alien peoples on the Mountain of Duca.* There came and lived in one of those caves Elpidius, a Cappadocian, subsequently deemed worthy of the priesthood, a member of the monastery of the most excellent Timothy, the rural bishop of Cappadocia. This Elpidius demonstrated such abstinence in his spiritual discipline that he put everybody in the shade.

*Josh 10:16

2. He lived for twenty-five years eating only on Sunday and Saturday; by night he stood singing. The majority of the brotherhood lived close by with him in the middle like a queen bee (I too lived with him), and thus he made the mountain

a city.[31] It was possible to see various ways of life there. A scorpion once stung this Elpidius when he was singing at night with us singing along. He trod on it without changing his position and paid no attention to the pain from the scorpion.

3. One day there was a brother who had a vine cutting. While sitting on the side of the mountain, Elpidius took it and heaped up soil as though planting it, although it was not the season. It grew so well that it became a vine protecting the church. Together with him, a person worthy of mention named Ænesius achieved perfection, and also Eustathios his brother. Elpidius advanced so far in *apatheia* that his body was macerated to the extent that the sun shone through his bones.

4. The story is told by the serious disciples of Elpidius that for twenty-five years he never turned toward the west, because the summit of the mountain overshadowed the door of the cave; nor did he ever see the sun after the sixth hour when it had reached its zenith and was declining toward the west, nor the stars rising in the west. Once he had gone into the cave he did not come down from the mountain until he was buried.

49. SISINNIUS

1. {There was a disciple of this Elpidius, Sisinnius by name, with a slave's fortune at birth but free in the faith, originally from Cappadocia. These

[31] See Vita A 8.2: "he made the desert a city of spiritual discipline," 14.7: "the desert became a city of monks," and 41.4: "the desert has been filled with monks."

things too should be pointed out for the glory of Christ, who makes us free and leads us to true nobility. After Sisinnius had spent six or seven years with Elpidius, he sequestered himself in a tomb, and for three years he continued in that tomb offering prayers. He neither sat nor lay down by night or day; nor did he step outside. He was deemed worthy of a spiritual gift against demons.

2. He has now returned to his homeland and has been deemed worthy of the priesthood. He has gathered together a community of men and women; by his devout way of life he has both driven out his own masculine desire and silenced the femininity of the women by continence, with the result that the Scripture was fulfilled: "In Christ Jesus there is neither male nor female."* He is also hospitable, even though he is devoid of possessions, to the reproof of the rich who do not share.}

*Gal 3:28

50. GADDANA

I made the acquaintance of an elderly person of Palestine named Gaddana, who lived an outdoor life in the places around the Jordan. In their zeal some Jews once set upon him in the places around the Dead Sea. They drew their swords and came at him, and this is what happened: when the sword was being lifted up with the intention of striking Gaddana, the hand of the one who had drawn the sword was dried up, and the sword fell from the right hand of him who held it.

51. ELIJAH

Elijah* too was living in the same places, alone in a cave, leading a very devout life alone, lawfully abiding. One day he ran short of bread, for very many brothers had come by, his place being on a thoroughfare. He assured us, "Despondent at the situation, I went into my cell and found three loaves. After twenty persons had eaten as much as they wanted, one of the loaves remained, and it lasted me for twenty-five days."

*see Monks 7

52. SABAS

{There was a worldling named Sabas, originally from Jericho, who had a wife and who was so devoted to monks that he would go around the cells and the desert by night setting a bushel of dates and a sufficient quantity of vegetables outside each monastery (because the ascetics in the Jordan region do not eat bread). One day a lion met him; he seized it and forced it a mile away; then he came back, took his ass, and went his way.}[32]

53. ABRAM

There was a man called Abram, an Egyptian by birth, who lived a most rough and savage life in the wilderness. Troubled in his mind by inappropriate conceit, he came into the church and

[32] This last sentence is ambiguous; it could mean that Sabas was seized and dragged by the lion rather than that Sabas dragged the lion.

contended with the priests, saying, "I was ordained priest by Christ last night: accept me as one exercising priesthood." The fathers removed him from the desert and brought him to a more earthly and less distinctive lifestyle; thus they cured him of his arrogance, bringing him to an awareness of his own sickness; he had been made a plaything by the demon.

54. HOLY MELANIA (AGAIN)

1. I briefly related some things about the wondrous and holy Melania above; nevertheless I will now weave the rest into the narrative. It is not for me to relate how much property she disposed of in holy zeal, as though she were burning with fire, even for those living in Persia. Nobody escaped her benevolence, east or west, north or south.

2. For thirty-seven years while living abroad she supported churches, monasteries, aliens, and prisons with her own resources—her own agents, her relatives, and her son himself furnishing her with funds. She who persevered for so long in a foreign country and possessed not a span of land was not drawn back by a desire to see her son. A longing for her only son did not divert her from her love for Christ,

3. but by her prayers the young man achieved the summit of education and manners. He made an illustrious marriage and became one of the worldly nobility. He had two children. Many years later she heard about the condition of her granddaughter, that she was married and had chosen to renounce the world. Fearing that her children might give

way to the influence of bad teaching, heresy, or evil living, at the age of sixty the old woman put herself aboard a ship and sailed away from Caesarea, arriving at Rome twenty days later.

4. There she met that most blessed and notable man Apronian,* who was a pagan; him she instructed and turned into a Christian. She persuaded him to live in continence with his own wife, who was her niece; she was called Avita. She confirmed her own granddaughter Melania in the faith and with her Pinian,* her husband. She also instructed Albina, her daughter-in-law, her son's wife, and, arranging for them all to sell their property, she led them out of Rome and brought them into the noble and peaceful harbor of life.

*see *Lausiac History* 41.5

*see *Lausiac History* 62.2, 7

5. Thus she fought as with wild beasts against all those of senatorial rank and their respectable wives who were obstructing the renunciation of her remaining houses. She would say to them, "Children, it was written four hundred years ago, 'It is the last hour.'* Why do you linger over the vanity of life? Perchance the days of Antichrist will arrive and you will no longer have the benefit of your wealth and ancestral benefits."

*1 John 2:18

6. She set them all free and led them into the monastic life. She instructed Publicola, her younger son, and took him into Sicily; she sold everything that remained to her, took the price, and came to Jerusalem, sharing out her substance. Then, within forty days, she died at a good old age and in the most profound humility, leaving a monastery in Jerusalem and provision for its maintenance.

7. After all these people had left Rome a barbaric hurricane mentioned in prophecies of old

*Alaric sacked Rome in 410; see *Oracula Sibyllina* 8:165

fell upon Rome* and did not even leave the bronze statues in the Forum. Everything was devastated with barbaric frenzy and delivered to destruction, and Rome, enhanced over 1200 years, became a ruin. Then they who had been instructed but had withstood the instruction glorified God, who persuaded the unbelieving by a change in fortunes that when all others had been taken prisoner, only those families had been saved, they having become an offering to the Lord through the zeal of Melania.

55. [SILVANIA]

1. It came about that we traveled together from Jerusalem to Egypt escorting that holy woman the blessed Silvania, sister-in-law of the prefect Rufinus. Among others, Jovinus was with us, then a deacon, now bishop of the church at Ascalon, a devout and learned man. A severe heat wave came upon us; when we touched on Pelusium, Jovinus happened to take a basin and wash his hands and feet meticulously in very cold water. After he had washed, he reposed on a fleece laid out on the ground.

2. Approaching him as a wise mother would her own son, Silvania reproved him for his softness, saying, "At your age, when your blood is still hot, how dare you cherish your flesh like that, regardless of the harm it can cause? Believe me, I am sixty years of age, and apart from the tips of my hands, neither my feet nor my face nor any one of my limbs ever touched water. I have suffered a variety of illnesses, and, although the phy-

sicians constrained me, I refused to give my body the usual care. I did not repose on a bed or travel anywhere in a litter."

3. She became a very learned woman, so enamored of the Word that she turned night into day, going through every writing of the old commentators, including {Origen,} Gregory, Stephen, Pierios, Basil, and two hundred and fifty thousand [lines] by other most serious writers. And she did not just read them casually; she laboriously read each volume over seven or eight times. Thus, set free of false teaching, she was able to fly up in the grace of the words with better hope, making herself a spiritual bird flying up to Christ.

56. OLYMPIA[33]

1. After Sylvania and walking in her footsteps came the most revered and zealous Olympia, following her in knowledge. She was the daughter of the Count Seleucus, the granddaughter of the former prefect Ablabius and (for a few days) the fiancée of Nebridius, sometime prefect of Constantinople, but she was the wife of no man. She is said to have died a spinster but spouse to the word of truth.

2. She gave away all her possessions, distributing them among the poor, and small by no means were the struggles she sustained for the truth. She instructed many women in the faith, spoke

[33] Born ca. 368, Olympia was briefly married in 384 to Nebridius, who died the following year. John Chrysostom wrote several letters to her when he was in exile.

respectfully of priests, honored bishops, and was deemed worthy of having made a confession on behalf of the truth. She died in such a way, migrating to the Lord while struggling on God's behalf, that the inhabitants of Constantinople judge her life to be among those of the confessors.[34]

57. CANDIDA AND GELASIA

1. After Olympia, as though reflecting her in a mirror, was the blessed Candida, daughter of the general Trajan.* She lived a fitting life and achieved the very summit of sanctity, honoring churches and bishops. She instructed her own daughter in the vocation of virginity, then sent her to Christ, the gift of her own womb. She subsequently followed in her daughter's footsteps by her temperance and distribution of money.

*duke of Egypt ca. 370, killed at Adrianople in 378

2. I have personally known Olympia to spend the whole night laboring, grinding with her own hands, to subject the body, explaining, "Since fasting is insufficient, I am providing it with a working vigil as an ally to break down the insolence of Esau."* She abstained completely from what had blood and life in it, but she did take some fish and vegetables with oil on a feast day. Otherwise she lived out her days satisfied with diluted vinegar and dried bread.

*Heb 12:16; Gen 25:25-34

3. In her footsteps zealously trod the most devout Gelasia, the daughter of a tribune, who also piously bore the yoke of virginity. This virtue is re-

[34] Feast day: July 24 (SynaxCP 841.7–842.11). Much was made of the fact that she was both widow and virgin.

lated of her: the sun never went down on her grievance against a slave, a handmaid, or anybody else.

58. THOSE AT ANTINOË[35]

1. Having spent four years at Antinoë in the Thebaid, in so much time I became acquainted with the monasteries that are there. About twelve hundred men are living round about the city, existing by the labor of their own hands and in strictest spiritual discipline. Among them are those who have withdrawn into caves in the rocks and have shut themselves in. Among them is one Solomon, a most gentle and sensible man who has the spiritual gift of patient endurance. He used to say that he had been in the cave for fifty years,[36] providing for himself by the work of his hands and learning the entire Holy Scripture.

2. Dorotheos the priest was living in another cave, a man of superlative excessive goodness and blameless life who was deemed worthy of the priesthood, which he exercised on behalf of the brothers in the caves. On one occasion the granddaughter of Melania the great, Melania the younger—of whom I will speak later on—sent five hundred pieces of

[35] Antinoë, the metropolis of the Thebaid (Monks 7.1), is located a little over six miles south of Beni Hasan at a village called Sheikh Abada, which sits in a lovely setting amid palm trees on the east bank of the Nile. Little is known of this Pharaonic town founded by the emperor Hadrian on October 30, AD 130. Legend has it that it was built in honor of Antinus, who threw himself into the Nile to save that emperor.

[36] "He was famous for having spent seventy years in the terrible desert: No description can do justice to that rugged desert in the mountain where he dwelt" (Monks 7.1).

gold to this priest, asking him to use it in the service of the brothers who were there. But he only took three of them; the rest he sent to Diocles the anchorite, a very learned man, with the words, "Brother Diocles is wiser than I am; he can administer this sum without causing harm—for he understands which ones rightly deserve to be given assistance; these are enough for me."

3. This Diocles was drawn to grammar at first but later devoted himself to philosophy; then, in due course, with grace drawing him on, when he became twenty-eight years of age he rejected secular learning and swore allegiance to Christ; he has been in the caves for thirty-five years. He would tell us, "The mind that distances itself from the thought of God becomes either a beast or a demon." When we inquired into the meaning of what he said, he would tell us, "The mind that distances itself from the thought of God inevitably falls into either lust or anger," and he would say that lust was beastly, anger demonic.

4. When I objected, saying, "How can the human mind be perpetually with God?" he would say, "In whatever thought or deed the soul is devout and godly, it is with God."

Adjacent to him there lived Capiton, a former brigand, who had completed fifty years in the caves four miles from the city of Antinoë and who never came down from his cave, not even as far as the River Nile. He said that he was not yet able to encounter crowds because the adversary was still at war with him.

5. In addition to these we saw another anchorite, also living in a cave like them. Deluded by a

mania for vainglory through his own dreams, he in turn used to make fun of those who are deceived: "He who follows after the winds. . . ."[37] He did indeed have temperance so far as his body was concerned through his old age and the passage of time, perhaps also from vainglory, but his ability to think clearly was ruined by an excess of vainglory.

59. AMMAS TALIS AND TAÔR

1. There are twelve monasteries for women in that city of Antinoë. I made the acquaintance of Amma Talis, an old woman who has spent eighty years under spiritual discipline, according to herself and her neighbors. Sixty young women living with her loved her so much that no key exists to the courtyard of the monastery, as at other monasteries: they are held there by their love of her. The old woman has attained such a degree of *apatheia* that when I came in and sat down, she came and sat down beside me and put her hands on my shoulders in exceeding familiarity.

2. In this monastery is a holy woman, a disciple of hers—Taôr is her name—who has been in the monastery for thirty years. She is ever unwilling to accept a new tunic, a shawl, or sandals, saying, "I am not in need—lest I be forced to go hence." All the others come forward in the church to receive communion on Sunday while this one stays in the monastery, dressed in rags, sitting at her work that

[37] An oblique reference to Sir 34:1-2: "Vain and false hopes are for one void of understanding, and dreams give wings to fools, as one who catches at a shadow and follows after the wind."

never ceases. Her face was so lovely that even the most obdurate of men would be beguiled by her beauty except that she had an overpowering guard in her continence, as with her modesty she drove the licentious eye to respect and fear.

60. COLLUTHUS, VIRGIN AND MARTYR

1. There was another woman living near me, but I did not see her face, for they said she had never come out since she renounced the world. Having spent sixty years in spiritual discipline together with her mother superior, she was eventually about to depart this life. The martyr of that region, Colluthus by name, stood by her and said to her, "Today you are going to travel to the lord-and-master and to see all the saints. Come and share a meal with us at the martyr's shrine." Rising early, she dressed herself, and taking bread, oil, and some vegetables in a basket of her own, she came out after so many years and went off to the martyr's shrine and prayed.

2. Watching for that part of the whole day when there was nobody inside, she sat down and called on the martyr, saying, "Holy Colluthus, bless my provisions and accompany me with your prayers." When she had eaten, she prayed again, then went back home at sundown. She gave a commentary on the prophet Amos by Clement of the *Stromateis*[38] to her mother [superior] with the words, "Give this to the bishop in exile and say to him, 'Pray for me, for I am going on a journey' "—and she died

[38] I.e., "The Miscellany," Clement of Alexandria, ca. 150–ca. 215.

that very night with no fever or headache, having prepared herself for burial.

61. MELANIA THE YOUNGER

1. Since I promised above to give an account of the [grand]child of Melania, I shall perforce pay what is owing. It would be a travesty to look down on her youth in body and cast away such virtue uncommemorated when she artlessly and by far outclassed many an aged and zealous old woman. Her parents strongly encouraged her to marry one of the leading citizens of Rome, but she was always influenced by what her grandmother had to say, to the point that she could not resign herself to marriage.

2. After the two sons born to her both died, her hatred of marriage became so great that she said to her husband, Pinian, the son of Severus, sometime prefect,* "If you chose to live under spiritual discipline together with me according to the word of continence, I would acknowledge you as lord-and-master of my life. If that seems burdensome for you who are young, take everything I own and set my body free so I may fulfill my godly yearning, inheriting the zeal of the grandmother whose name I bear.

*of Rome

3. "For if God had willed us to produce children he would not have taken away from me in an untimely manner those I bore." After they had argued the matter at considerable length, God took pity on the young man and inspired him with zeal for renunciation so that the Scripture might be fulfilled in them: "What do you know, wife, whether you will save [your] husband?"* And so, married at thirteen

*1 Cor 7:16

and having lived with her husband for seven years, she renounced the world when she was twenty. She started by donating her silk clothing for the altars, the holy Olympia having done likewise.

4. The remaining silks she cut up and made into various church furnishings. Entrusting the silver and gold to a priest named Paul, a monk of Dalmatia, she sent ten thousand pieces of gold across the sea to the east, to Egypt and the Thebaid, then ten thousand to Antioch and its hinterland, fifteen thousand to Palestine, and ten thousand to the island churches and to people in exile, providing personally in similar fashion for the churches in the west,

5. having snatched all these for God and four times as many out of the mouth of Alaric the lion by her personal faith. She set free eight thousand slaves who desired it; the rest, who did not want freedom, chose to serve her brother. She assigned them all to him to take, at three pieces of gold per head. She sold her properties in Spain, Aquitaine, Tarragon, and the provinces of Gaul. Leaving only those in Sicily, Campania, and Africa for herself, she held onto those for the maintenance of monasteries.

6. This was her prudence concerning the burden of riches, and this was her spiritual discipline. She would eat once in two days, even once in more than five days at first, appointing herself to the daily duty of one of her own maidservants, whom she also made her fellows in spiritual discipline. She also has her mother with her, Albina, under similar spiritual discipline, and she is distributing her personal fortune in her own way too. They are

living out in the countryside, now in Sicily, now in Campania, with fifteen eunuchs and sixty young women, both enslaved and free.

7. Likewise Pinian her husband is living with thirty monks, reading and passing his time in tending the garden and having godly conversations. He did us no small honor when quite a number of us went off to Rome on behalf of the blessed Bishop John [Chrysostom], refreshing us with hospitality and very generous provisions for the journey. With great joy they are cultivating the life eternal with the God-given tasks of the best way of life.

62. PAMMACHIUS

A relative of theirs, a former proconsul, Pammachius by name,* also renounced the world and lived the excellent life. He distributed all his wealth, some of it while he was living; some of it he left to the poor when he was dying. So too did a certain Macarius, sometime vicar,* and Constantius, who had been counsellor to the prefects of Italy. These were illustrious and highly educated men who had attained the highest level of godliness. I believe they are still living and pursuing the excellent life in spiritual discipline.

*a senator and a former colleague of Jerome, d. 409

*i.e., of an imperial diocese

63. THE HOLY WOMAN WHOSE GUEST WAS THE BLESSED ATHANASIUS

1. I made the acquaintance of a holy woman in Alexandria who was seventy years old when I met her. All the clergy attested that when she was

young, about twenty years old, and exceedingly beautiful, she was sequestered on account of her beauty lest she bring disgrace (arising from an expectation) on anybody. It came about in the time of the emperor Constantius that the Arians gained the confidence of Eusebius the chamberlain. They began plotting against the blessed Athanasius, bishop of Alexandria. Bearing false witness, they alleged wicked things against him. So, to avoid being judged by a corrupt tribunal, he ran away—for he could not trust anybody, neither relative nor friend nor clergy nor anybody else.

2. When the prefect's agents suddenly entered the episcopal residence in search of Athanasius, he, taking his thin tunic and his hooded cloak, fled to this holy woman in the middle of the night. Alarmed by this occurrence, she was afraid, so he said to her, "Since I am being sought by the Arians and am being falsely accused of wicked things, in order not to acquire an irrational reputation and to cast into sin those who are seeking to punish me, I ran away.

3. "For this very night God revealed to me, 'You will be kept safe by none other if not by her.'" In great joy she cast every argument aside and became wholly on the Lord's side. For six years, as long as Constantius was living, she hid that most holy one, washing his feet, attending to his excrement, and supplying his every need. She borrowed and provided books for him, and for six years not a soul in Alexandria knew where the blessed Athanasius was living.

*AD 361

4. When the death of Constantius* was announced and it came to Athanasius's ears, to the

amazement of everybody he appeared once again in the church by night, vested appropriately, and they saw him as a living person returned from the dead. He made excuses to his sincere friends: "I did not take refuge with you for this reason: so that you could swear in good faith. Also, because of the searches, I fled to her whom nobody could suspect, she being young and beautiful. Thus I have achieved two things: her salvation (for I was of benefit to her) and my own reputation."

64. JULIANA

1. Then too there was Juliana, a holy woman at Caesarea in Cappadocia, said to be highly educated and most faithful. For two years she sheltered as her guest the writer Origen,* running away from the uprising of the pagans. She cared for the man at her own expense, personally waiting on him. I found this written in a very old book of poetry in Origen's own hand: *ca. 185–ca. 254

2. "I found this book at the home of Juliana, the holy woman in Caesarea, when I was in hiding with her, and she said she received it from Symmachus, the interpreter of the Jews."

65. THE STORY OF HIPPOLYTUS[39]

1. In another very old book composed by Hippolytus, the acquaintance of the apostles,* I found *d. 235

[39] = Bibliotheca 1318h; George Monachus, *Chronicon*, 2 vols., ed. C. de Boor (Leipzig: Teubner, 1904), 479.13–480.14; Nicephorus Callistus Xanthopoulos, HE 7.13.

a story like this: There was a most noble and beautiful spinster in the city of Corinth, conserving her virginity in spiritual discipline. This was in the time of the persecutions, and they defamed her in those days before the then-magistrate (who was a pagan), accusing her of blaspheming the state of affairs and the emperors and of speaking ill of the idols. Those however who traded in such things were praising her beauty too.

2. Now the magistrate was a womanizer; he gladly accepted the defamation, pricking up his horse-like ears. Although he employed every device to coerce her, he was unable to do so, but, angry though he was with her, he did not impose a punishment or a beating on her. He put her in a brothel, instructing the one in charge of the women, "Take this one and bring me three pieces of gold each day from her earnings." Anxious to make money for himself, he made her available to those who wanted her. When the woman hunters became aware of this, they were in constant attendance at the workshop of destruction, paying their money and seducing her with words.

3. She, however, earnestly entreated them and begged them, saying, "I have some kind of ulcer in a secret part that stinks abominably, and I am afraid that you will come to hate me. Excuse me for a few days; then I will be in your power and you shall have me *gratis*." She was beseeching God with supplications during those days; hence, when God observed her continence, he inspired a young man, an intelligent and handsome imperial officer, with a burning desire to die. Off he went, feigning licentiousness, and came to the person who cared

for the women late in the evening. Giving him five pieces of gold, he said to him, "Let me stay the night with her."

4. When he came into her private quarters he said to her, "Get up and save yourself." He undressed her and changed her clothing for his own, the shirts, the mantle, and all the men's clothes, and said to her, "Go out wrapped up in the border of the mantle." Making the sign of the cross, out she went and was saved, pure and unadulterated. Next day the stratagem became known; the young man was handed over to the magistrate and thrown to wild beasts so the demon might be put to shame in that he was martyr twice over: once for himself, once for that blessed woman.

66. COUNT VERUS

1. At Ancyra* in Galatia, in the city itself, I met a highly distinguished count named Verus and enjoyed a protracted experience of him and at the same time of Bosporia, his wife. They had attained such a degree of kindly hope as to leave their children out of their reckoning, in their action looking to what is to come. They were spending the income of their lands on the indigent; they had two daughters and four sons but gave them not so much as a vine cutting except for dowries to the girls, saying, "Everything will be yours after our death." They were collecting the rents from properties and dividing them among town and country churches.

*now Ankara

2. This virtuous deed exists among others too: there was a famine. Moved with compassion, they restored heretics to orthodoxy by setting up their

granaries for the support of the poor in many a village. And something else: taking up the most modest and simple clothing, they wore very inexpensive garments and lived on the simplest diet, practicing godly continence. For the most part they associated with the countryside, shunning the cities lest by enjoying themselves in company they might imbibe a little of the urban tumult, abandoning their intention.

67. MAGNA

1. In that city of Ancyra there are many other spinsters, about two thousand or more, also some women distinguished by their continence and decency. Preeminent among them for godliness was Magna, a most noble woman; I do not know whether to call her spinster or widow. Constrained to marry a husband by her own mother, she got the better of him and contrived (as most people say) to remain untouched.

2. When he died a little later she gave herself entirely to God, appropriately administering her own houses, living a life of intense spiritual discipline and chastity. Her relations with others were such that bishops too revered her for her outstanding godliness. With the surplus income that remained she provided for the needs of hospices, the poor, and traveling bishops, never ceasing to labor in secret herself and always using highly trusted slaves, without absenting herself from the church by night.

68. THE BENEVOLENT MONK

1. Likewise we found in that city a monk who had served in the army for a short time and who chose not to receive ordination to the priesthood. He has been under spiritual discipline for twenty years with this way of life; he lives with the bishop of the city, and such is his philanthropy and benevolence that he goes around at night taking pity on the needy.

2. He pays no heed to whether they are in prison or hospital, rich or poor; he brings succor to all, offering words of compassion to those who know no compassion. Some he protects, some he calms down, providing others with clothing and what their bodies require. What usually happens in all large cities happens here too: a multitude of sick persons lies in the church porch (married and single), begging their daily bread.

3. Now one day it came about that the wife of one of these people was giving birth in the porch, in winter, in the middle of the night. Hearing her crying out in her labor pains, he abandoned his customary prayers, came out, and saw her. As he found nobody to serve as a midwife he took her place himself, not at all disgusted by the defilement that accompanies women in childbirth; his benevolence had made him insensitive to it.

4. The type of clothing he wears is not worth a penny, and his food is of like value. He is not persistently bending over a writing tablet, since his philanthropic activities take him away from reading. If any one of the brothers gives him a book, he immediately sells it, saying to those who are laughing at him, "How can I persuade my Master

that I have learned his craft if I do not sell him himself in carrying out his craft?"*

*see the tale of Serapion Sindonios, *Lausiac History* 37, etc.

69. THE SPINSTER WHO FELL AND REPENTED

1. An ascetic spinster living with two others practiced spiritual discipline for nine or ten years. Then she was seduced by and fell with a cantor, became pregnant, and bore a child. When her hatred for him who had seduced her reached the boiling point, she had a profound change of heart; she became repentant to the point of starving herself to death right away, killing herself with hunger.

2. In prayer she begged of God, saying, "O great God who bears the evils of all creation and who does not wish the death and destruction of those who are at fault, if you want me to be saved, show me your wondrous works like this: gather in the fruit of my sin that I brought into the world, so that I do not use the rope or throw myself down." She was heard praying these things—for not long afterward, the child she had borne expired.

3. From that day on she never again met the one who had captivated her. She subjected herself to the most severe fasting, for thirty years serving sick and mutilated women. She so won God over that it was revealed to one of the holy priests, "So-and-so has pleased me more by her repentance than by her virginity." I am writing this so that we do not look down on those who sincerely repent.

70. A LECTOR FALSELY ACCUSED[40]

1. The daughter of a priest at Caesarea in Palestine, a fallen spinster, was taught by her seducer falsely to accuse a certain lector of the city. When the pregnancy was somewhat advanced and she was questioned by her father, she accused the lector. The priest confidently brought the matter to the bishop. The bishop convened the clergy and had the lector summoned. The matter was thoroughly investigated; the lector did not confess when he was questioned by the bishop; how could he speak up about that which had not taken place?

2. Moved to anger, the bishop sternly said to him, "You are not confessing, wretch, miserable one, full of uncleanness?" The lector replied, "I have told it as it is; I am not responsible; I am innocent of a design against her. If you want to hear what did not happen, then: I did it." When he had said this, the bishop deposed the lector. Then the lector went and besought the bishop, saying, "Since then I have committed this fault, bid her to be given to me as wife, since I am no longer a cleric and she not a spinster."

3. So the bishop gave her to the lector under the impression that he was in love with her, and besides he could not break off his customary relations with her. The young man received her from both the bishop and her father—then put her into a women's monastery, beseeching the administrator of the sisterhood there to keep her until she went into labor. Shortly the time came for her to

[40] For similar stories see Macarius the Egyptian 1 (PG 65:257C–260B; APsys 15.39), PS 114, Bibliotheca 1450zs, zq.

give birth. When the critical time came there were groans, pangs, and throes, visions of the lower regions, but the child did not come forth.

4. The first day came and went, the second, the third, and the seventh, and the woman was going through hell from the pain; neither did she drink nor get any rest. She cried out saying, "Ah me, wretch that I am! I am in danger for having falsely accused that lector." The women went and told her father, but he was afraid of being condemned of being a false accuser and kept quiet for another two days. The young woman neither died nor gave birth. When the spinsters could bear her cries no longer, they ran and reported to the bishop, "For some days so-and-so has been confessing in her cries that she accused the lector falsely." Then he sent deacons to the lector, telling him, "Pray that she who falsely accused you might give birth."

5. For his part he neither gave them an answer nor opened his own door from the day he went in, praying to God. Her father came to the bishop again, and there was prayer in church, but even so she did not give birth. Then the bishop got up and went to the lector. He knocked at the door, went in to him, and said, "Get up, Eustathius; loose what you have bound."[41] And as soon as he knelt down with the bishop, the woman gave birth. This man's supplication and the persistence of his prayer were strong enough both to expose the false accusation and to chastise her who had made it, so that we

[41] The notion that only the one who bound can loosen (see Matt 18:18) occurs frequently in beneficial tales, e.g., Bibliotheca 1318z, 1322u, ua, v; 1449s, 2102d (Daniel of Scete 7), and PS 193, Anastasios the Sinaite C 18.

might learn to persevere in prayers and be aware of their power.

71. EPILOGUE

1. So then, I shall draw the discourse to a close after saying a few words about the brother who has been my companion from my youth until today.[42] Over a long stretch of time, I have perceived that he neither eats with passion nor fasts with passion, that (so far as I can tell) he has vanquished the passion for money and, for the most part, the passion for vainglory, also that he is satisfied with what is available. He does not dress himself up in clothing, he gives thanks when treated disrespectfully, he puts himself in danger for his sincere friends, and he has received testing from demons a thousand times and more, so that one day a demon even tried to make a pact with him, saying, "Agree with me to sin just once, and in this life I will bring you whatever woman you tell me to bring."

2. Then another time (as he told me), after wrestling with him again for fourteen nights and dragging him by the foot, the demon spoke aloud to the brother by night, saying, "Do not worship Christ, and I will not come near you." In reply, the brother said, "That is why I worship him, and I glorify and worship him ever more and more because you are totally disgusted." Although the brother had trod

[42] It is generally (but not universally) agreed that Palladius is here speaking of himself, as is Saint Paul in the passage from which the quotation in *Lausiac History* 71.4 (below) is taken.

the streets of 106 cities[43] and stayed for some time in most of them, by the mercy of God he had no experience of a woman, not even in a dream, except in battle with the demons.

3. I am aware of his having three times received the bread he needed from an angel. One day when he was in the remotest desert and did not even have a crumb, he found three warm loaves in his sheepskin. Another time too he found wine and loaves. Yet again he was aware of someone saying, "You are running short, so go and receive grain and oil from so-and-so." He went to the one to whom he had been sent and said to him, "Are you so-and-so?" "Yes," he said; "Somebody told you to receive thirty *modii* of grain and twelve *sextarii* of oil."

*2 Cor 12:5

4. "On behalf of such a one I will glory,"* for the brother was such a one. I know that he often wept over folk who were in need and suffering penury; he would provide them with everything he possessed except for his flesh. I know that he also lamented over one who fell into sin and brought the one who had fallen to repentance by his tears. He once swore to me, "I besought God not to prompt anybody (especially one of the rich and mean) to give me anything when in need."

5. For my part, it is enough to have been deemed worthy to commemorate all these persons whose lives I have committed to writing. For it was not without the help of God that your mind was moved to charge me with the composition of this book and

[43] This phrase could mean *106 monastic communities*. See *Lausiac History* 48.2 and note.

to commit to writing the lives of these holy ones. You, most faithful servant of Christ, reading them with delight and taking their lives, their labors, and their so patient endurance as a manifestation of the resurrection, follow them eagerly, nourished by a noble hope as you see the days ahead of you becoming fewer than those behind.

6. Pray for me and keep yourself as I have known you since the consulate of Tatian* until today and as I found you again, appointed chamberlain of the most venerated bedchamber. He whose fear of God such a dignity (with its wealth and so much power) has not diminished, that person is dedicated to Christ—who heard from the devil, "All these will I give you if you will fall down and worship me."*

*AD 391

*Matt 4:9

Bibliography

Text of *Historia Lausiaca*

The Lausiac History of Palladius. Edited by Cuthbert Butler. 2 vols. Cambridge, UK: Cambridge University Press, 1898, 1904.

Les Moines du désert. Translated by Les sœurs carmelites de Mazille. Paris: Desclée de Brouwer, 1981.

Palladio, La Storia Lausiaca. Edited by G. J. M. Bartelink. Translated by Marino Barchiesi. Milan: Fondazione Lorenza Valla and Libri Mondadori, 1974.

Primary Texts

The Life of Antony

Athanase d'Alexandrie. *Vie d'Antoine*. Edited and translated by G. J. M. Bartelink. SCh 400. Paris: Éditions du Cerf, 1994.

The Life of Antony: The Coptic Life and the Greek Life. Translated by Tim Vivian and A. N. Athanasakis. CS 202. Kalamazoo, MI: Cistercian Publications, 2003.

Apophthegmata Patrum

The Anonymous Sayings of the Desert Fathers. Edited and translated by John Wortley. Cambridge, UK: Cambridge University Press, 2013.

Apophthegmata patrum, collection alphabetica. Edited by Jean-Baptiste Cotelier. Monumenta Ecclesiae Graecae, vol. 1. Paris, 1647. Reedited by J.-P. Migne. PG 65:71–440.

The Book of the Elders: Sayings of the Desert Fathers; The Systematic Collection. Translated by John Wortley. CS 240. Collegeville, MN: Cistercian Publications, 2012.

Give Me a Word: The Alphabetical Sayings of the Desert Fathers. Translated by John Wortley. Yonkers, NY: St Vladimir's Seminary Press, 2014.

Les Apophtegmes des Pères: collection systématique. Edited and translated by Jean-Claude Guy. 3 vols. SCh 387, 474, and 498. Paris: Éditions du Cerf, 1993, 2003, 2005.

Les Sentences des Pères du Désert: Collection alphabétique. Translated by Dom Lucien Regnault. Solesmes: Bellefontaine, 1966.

Les Sentences des Pères du Désert, Série des Anonymes. Translated by Dom Lucien Regnault. Solesmes: Bellefontaine, 1985.

Other Travelogues

Enquête sur les Moines d'Egypte. Translated by André-Jean Festugière. In *Les Moines d'Orient*, 4/1. Paris: Les Éditions du Cerf, 1964.

Historia Monachorum in Ægypto. Edited by André-Jean Festugière. Subsidia Hagiographica 53. Brussels: Société des Bollandistes, 1971.

The Lives of the Desert Fathers. Translated by Norman Russell. Oxford, UK, and Kalamazoo, MI: Mowbray/Cistercian Publications, 1981. [A new translation by John Wortley is forthcoming.]

Moschos, John. *Fioretti des moines d'orient, Jean Moschos: Le Pré spirituel.* Translated by Jean Bouchet with an introduction and notes by Vincent Déroche. Paris: Migne, 2006.

———. *Pratum Spirituale.* Edited by J.-P. Migne (after Fronto Ducaeus and J.-B. Cotelier), with the Latin translation of Ambrose Traversari. PG 87:2851–3112.

———. *The Spiritual Meadow.* Translated by John Wortley. CS 139. Kalamazoo, MI: Cistercian Publications, 1992.

General Works

Chadwick, Henry. *The Early Church.* The Penguin History of the Church, vol. 1. London: Penguin, 1963.

Chitty, J. Derwas. *The Desert a City: An Introduction to the Study of Egyptian and Palestinian Monasticism Under the Christian Empire.* Oxford, UK: Basil Blackwell and Mott Ltd., 1966. Reprint Crestwood, NY: St. Vladimir's Seminary Press, 1977.

Chryssavgis, John. *In the Heart of the Desert: The Spirituality of the Desert Fathers and Mothers.* Bloomington, IN: World Wisdom, Inc., 2003.

Görg, Peter H. *The Desert Fathers: Saint Anthony and the Beginnings of Monasticism.* San Francisco: Ignatius Press, 2011.

Gould, Graham. *The Desert Fathers on Monastic Community.* Oxford, UK: Clarendon Press, 1993.

Guillaument, Antoine. *Études sur la spiritualité de l'Orient Chrétien.* Spiritualité Orientale no. 66. Bégrolles-en-Mauges (France): Abbaye de Bellefontaine, 1996.

———. "Le Désert des Kellia, un grand site monastique." In *Déserts chrétiens d'Égypte*, edited by Myriam Orban, 29–45. Nice: Culture Sud, 1993.

Guy, Jean-Claude. *Recherches sur la tradition grecque des Apophthegmata Patrum*. 2nd ed. Subsidia hagiographica 36. Brussels: Société des Bollandistes, 1962.

Harmless, William. *Desert Christians: An Introduction to the Literature of Early Monasticism*. Oxford, UK: Oxford University Press, 2004.

Regnault, Dom Lucien. *La Vie quotidienne des Pères du Désert en Égypte au IVe siècle*. Paris: Hachette, 1990.

Williams, Rowan. *Silence and Honey Cakes: The Wisdom of the Desert*. Oxford, UK: Lion Books, 2004.

CPSIA information can be obtained
at www.ICGtesting.com
Printed in the USA
FSHW011710210921
84915FS

9 780879 072520